X-PLANES 3

NORTH AMERICAN X-15

Peter E. Davies

SERIES EDITOR TONY HOLMES

OSPREY PUBLISHING
Bloomsbury Publishing Plc

Kemp House, Chawley Park, Cumnor Hill, Oxford OX2 9PH, UK
29 Earlsfort Terrace, Dublin 2, Ireland
1385 Broadway, 5th Floor, New York, NY 10018, USA
Email: info@ospreypublishing.com
www.ospreypublishing.com

OSPREY is a trademark of Osprey Publishing Ltd

First published in Great Britain in 2017

A CIP catalogue record for this book is available from the British Library.

Print ISBN: 978 1 4728 1991 8
ePDF: 978 1 4728 1992 5
ePub: 978 1 4728 1993 2
XML: 978 1 4728 2646 6

Edited by Tony Holmes
Artwork by Adam Tooby
Index by Mark Swift
Originated by PDQ Media, Bungay, UK
Printed and bound in India by Replika Press Private Ltd.

22 23 24 25 26   10 9 8 7 6 5 4

The Woodland Trust
Osprey Publishing supports the Woodland Trust, the UK's leading woodland conservation charity.

www.ospreypublishing.com
To find out more about our authors and books visit our website. Here you will find extracts, author interviews, details of forthcoming events and the option to sign-up for our newsletter.

Acknowledgements
I am most grateful to Paul Crickmore and Terry Panopalis for the use of photographs from their collections

Front Cover
NASA pilot Joseph Walker flies the third X-15, 56-6672 (nicknamed *THE LITTLE JOE II)*, on August 22, 1963. Launched from NB-52A 52-0003, which was flown by Majs Russell Bement and Ken Lewis, at 1006hrs, Walker made one of the series of high-altitude flights that were a focus of the X-15 program in 1963. Three of the four flights that qualified the pilots for astronaut status (for flights above 328,000ft/62 miles) were by Walker. Climbing at 4,000ft/sec at a 48-degree angle, the rocket fuel in Walker's X-15 burned out after 85.5 seconds. 56-6672 then coasted on up to 354,000ft/67.1 miles above the Earth, exceeding Mach 5.58 (3,794mph). This remained the altitude record for a winged aircraft for 41 years until Brian Binnie broke it in Dick Rutan's SpaceShipOne on October 4, 2004. Having peaked out at the top of his climb, Walker had to re-enter the atmosphere in a controlled glide and return to land at Edwards Air Force Base (AFB) at the end of an 11 minutes 8 seconds flight covering 305 ground miles, but over 67 miles vertically. Using manual controls, he held the aircraft at a 25-degree angle of attack as it descended from space in a 45-degree arc at up to 5,500ft/sec. At 70,000ft Walker pulled up into level flight, subjecting his body to 5g pressure that pooled his blood painfully in his limbs. (Cover artwork by Adam Tooby)

XPLANES
CONTENTS

CHAPTER ONE

BEATING THE HEAT

A metal ball weighing 184lb was detected in a low Earth orbit on October 4, 1957 by amateur radio operators worldwide, to their considerable surprise. Although it was able only to signal its presence through its one-watt radio transmitter, OKB-1's Sputnik 1 satellite transformed America's perception of Soviet technology. It triggered anxiety about the "missile gap" between the Soviet Union and the USA and signaled the start of the "space race."

The R-7 Semyorka rocket that launched the world's first artificial satellite was thought to be based on a formidable intercontinental ballistic missile (ICBM), possibly one of many threatening the West. Sputnik 1 had pre-empted President Dwight D. Eisenhower's announced intention to launch an American artificial satellite during the 1957–58 International Geophysical Year – ostensibly a time of international scientific cooperation. In fact, it was this announcement in July 1955 that had accelerated Soviet plans, including the design of larger 3,100lb satellites with military implications which the White House saw as the real threat.

However, although it seemed humiliating for America to have a Russian satellite regularly passing unchallenged over Washington, D.C., Moscow would have been surprised to learn in 1957 that American designers were initiating several very advanced projects. They included a successor to the USAF's imminent North American X-15 research aircraft. Project HYWARDS (Hypersonic Weapon and Research and Development Supporting System) conjectured a manned vehicle capable of speeds approaching Mach 18.

An enlarged version of the first supersonic aircraft, the X-1A reached Mach 2.44 in 1953, encountering severe stability problems at that speed. It ascended to a record 90,440ft the following year. Its Reaction Motors XLR-11 rocket engine was used for the early flights by the X-15. (USAF)

Harrison Storms (left) said that he "concentrated on stability and strength" in designing the X-15. When North American Aviation (NAA) won the Apollo space capsule contract it was a climax to his spectacular career, but he was made the scapegoat when three astronauts died in a capsule fire in January 1967. Sacked from NAA, Storms continued to work unofficially on the bid that secured the Space Shuttle contract for the company. He is seen here with Wernher von Braun, the founding father of rocket-powered flight. (NASA)

Among those who saw Sputnik as more than a Russian propaganda success was Harrison Storms at North American Aviation (NAA), who was seeking support for the X-15 manned hypersonic vehicle and would later help to give America the undoubted lead in space travel with the Apollo and Saturn V Moon landings. The term "hypersonic" implied speeds of Mach 5, (3,300mph or 5,000ft/sec). Many associated it with a "thermal barrier" – a point beyond which steel would melt. The notion of attaining such spectacular performance was generated over a decade before Sputnik. Influential designers such as Theodor von Kármán in America and Dennis Bancroft in England outlined 1,000mph aircraft in the early 1940s, and in Germany Werner von Braun's V2 ballistic missiles were regularly exceeding Mach 4. In 1944 Dr Eugen Sänger and Dr Irene Bredt argued that a hypersonic rocket-powered aircraft was technically possible.

NACA's (National Advisory Committee for Aeronautics) inclination to conceive such an aircraft increased following Sputnik and America's unique achievements with its early X-planes. In October 1947 Capt Chuck Yeager had made the world's first official supersonic flight in the rocket-powered Bell XS-1, ordered in March 1945. Bell Aircraft Corporation had already conceived a swept-wing, follow-up rocketplane, the X-2, to investigate the next "barrier" – extreme heat. As an aircraft re-entered denser air from very high altitude its energy was converted into heat, generating local airframe temperatures of up to 2,000 degrees F.

The X-2 had an unduly long gestation period, due mainly to propulsion problems, and both examples were destroyed in accidents before completing much heat research. However, in September 1956 it became the first aircraft to reach Mach 3, although pilot Mel Apt was lost in the process when the X-2 experienced uncontrollable pitch and yaw excesses and crashed. The first generation X-planes completed their work when Joe Walker made the final X-1E flight on November 6, 1958.

Together with the Douglas D-558, the eight Bell examples had validated the new practice of building pure research aircraft with no direct military application. They could explore flight regimes that could not be simulated accurately by the wind-tunnel testing and primitive computer technology of that time. Their courageous pilots' willingness to explore the unknown and push their aircraft to the limits had already yielded much research data that also validated the introduction of more advanced types to double existing speed and altitude records. At speeds above Mach 6 (one mile per second) they would have to encounter structural temperatures above 1,300 degrees F and maneuver safely in the airless void 50 miles above the Earth's surface. The renewed interest in developing manned aircraft to go ever higher and faster meant that the X-15, the hypersonic rocket-plane to achieve all those ambitions, took to the air only eight months after the last X-1 flight. It was to be one of the most remarkable, innovative and productive aircraft projects ever undertaken.

Among the first proposals for the new X-plane was a 1952 concept by David Stone of NACA to use a modified Bell X-2. It would have accelerated to supersonic speed before "launch" (impossible with existing carrier aircraft like the Boeing EB-50), with two solid-propellant JPL-4 Sergeant rocket boosters powering it to Mach 4.5 at 300,000ft. Stone also included a reaction control system releasing small jets of gas from the nose and wingtips to correct the aircraft's attitude in airless conditions where normal flying controls were ineffective. A similar system was tested in the X-1B and became vital equipment in the X-15 and many subsequent spaceflight ventures.

An earlier state-of-the-art NACA proposal by Hubert Drake and Robert Carman (who later worked on the X-15) involved an X-2 derivative and a larger supersonic carrier vehicle. Climbing to Mach 3 and 150,000ft, the carrier would launch the X-2-type plane which would soar to Mach 10 at 1,000,000ft altitude, or 189 miles. The ensuing debate, and earlier research by Sänger and Bredt and Bell's Robert J. Woods, led to a NACA panel meeting in February 1954 chaired by Hartley A. Soulé from its Langley laboratory where ideas were pooled on hypersonic flight, including X-2 derivatives and a thin-winged D-558-II Skyrocket. The panel rejected them all as being outdated and advocated a totally new design. NACA Langley's "thin wing" pioneer Robert Gilruth introduced the idea of a hypersonic aircraft to investigate re-entry to the upper atmosphere as an introduction to manned space flight.

An additional spur came from the USAF, which was considering similar research but for advanced weapons systems. Its "BoMi" (Bomber-Missile) and "RoBo" (Rocket-Bomber) studies, promoted by Bell Aircraft, used one of Sänger and Bredt's ideas that was developed by German rocket scientist Walter R. Dornberger, a Bell employee post-war. This envisaged a rocket-powered ionospheric research plane flying at an altitude of 50 to 75 miles and extending its range by "skipping" in and out of the atmosphere at hypersonic speed. Sänger's 92ft long Silbervogel (Silverbird) "Antipodal Bomber" of the late 1930s would have crossed half the world at 13,596mph, delivering 660lb of bombs on the USA en route. Its launcher was a static rocket booster track 1.8 miles long that released the aircraft at Mach 1.5 for it to ascend using its own powerful rocket motor.

This "skip-gliding" idea, originated in 1928, was fortunately abandoned by Nazi Germany but it was strongly supported by Woods and it eventually matured into Project Dyna-Soar/X-20 ("Dynamic-Soaring") in 1957. This 35ft-long piloted vehicle, launched by a Titan III ICBM booster, was designed mainly to explore techniques for re-entry to the atmosphere from orbital flight. Bell also devised

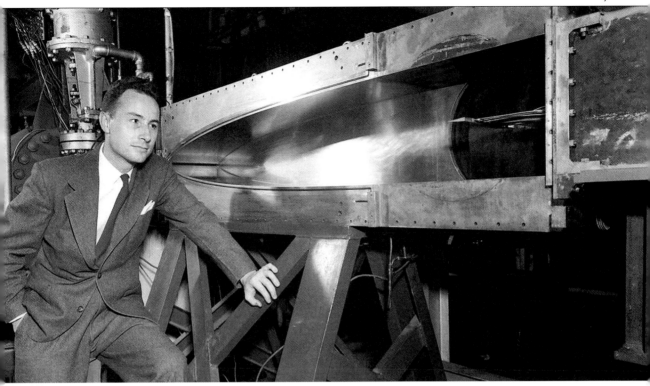

Hypersonic pioneer John V. Becker with NACA Langley's unique 11in diameter wind tunnel, which he instigated. It could generate airflow at Mach 6.9 for around 1.5 minutes as early as 1947, and it became the most important source of wind-tunnel data for the X-15. (NASA)

a two-stage, rocket-boosted Step II version with strategic bombing potential, skip-gliding for 5,000 miles, although the USAF favored a high-altitude reconnaissance variant. Step I Dyna-Soar was awarded to Boeing in November 1959 and construction began, but support waned as funding shifted to the Mercury and Gemini manned space programs and questions were raised about Dyna-Soar's small payload and high costs.

The project was terminated by Secretary of Defense Robert S. McNamara before its first flight, scheduled for mid-1965, but it generated considerable research and technology that assisted both the Space Shuttle and X-15 by providing equipment such as inertial guidance systems. Four pilots that had originally been prepared for the Dyna-Soar also went on to fly the X-15. Finally, some of the Dyna-Soar's intended functions, including orbital flight, were conferred upon projected developments of the X-15.

Following the 1954 panel meeting NACA Langley formed a research group led by John V. Becker, head of the organization's Compressibility Research Division, which included rocket expert Maxime A. Faget and aerodynamic heating specialist Norris F. Dow. Becker judged that "By 1954 we had reached a definite conclusion: the existing potentialities of these rocket-boosted aircraft could not be realized without major advances in all areas of aircraft design. In particular, the unprecedented problems of aerodynamic heating and high-temperature structures appeared to be so formidable that they were viewed as 'barriers' to hypersonic flight." He also noted that "The powerful new propulsion systems needed for aircraft flight beyond Mach 3 were identifiable in the large rocket engines being developed in the long-range missile program." Becker welcomed the "virtually unanimous support for hypersonic technology development" and was grateful that there was no competition in 1954 from other glamorous and expensive manned space projects. The project that produced the X-15 was, therefore, "born at what appears to be, in retrospect, the most propitious of all possible times for its promotion and approval."

Becker's panel drafted a design which presented the outline and specifications of the X-15. It was fairly conventional in appearance, with stubby wings and a cruciform tail assembly for added stability. Crucially, the design specified a new metal to "beat the heat" for most of the structure. Inconel-X, a chrome-nickel alloy produced by the International Nickel Corporation, combined with innovative heat-sink constructional techniques, was specified from the outset, although Richard Rhode at NACA Headquarters tried to veto it as it was "too critical a material." Weighing three times as much as aluminum alloys, it had been developed in the 1940s for small parts in jet engines. Stainless steel and titanium were also considered, but Inconel-X was clearly unrivalled in retaining its strength at extreme temperatures without the need for a "double wall" with insulation between inner and outer shells, as Bell proposed. It was clear that the Inconel-X skin would heat up at different rates depending on its position in the airframe, and this eventually required some highly innovative construction techniques.

More detailed work followed, with a study of operational objectives by NACA Dryden boss Walter Williams and an investigation of powerplant choices by the Lewis Flight Propulsion Laboratory. NACA's Ames and Langley Laboratories began work on aerodynamics and wind-tunnel testing of the basic Becker-group design models. The group also had to consider issues such as the pilot's two-minute exposure to weightlessness, problems of aircraft control and stability in airless conditions, aerodynamic heating up to 2,000 degrees F and flight profiles (particularly angle of attack) for atmospheric re-entry from a brief "space leap" climb above 100,000ft.

In order to avoid the early X-planes' longitudinal stability problems, it was assumed that a massive, thin, vertical stabilizer of roughly the same area as one wing would be needed to maintain directional stability at speeds up to Mach 7. However, Charles H. McClellan at NACA Langley proposed a smaller, wedge-shaped structure (and a similar ventral fin) with a sharp leading edge and a blunt trailing edge that could split and extend into two speed brakes to assist with re-entry. The latter were modified for the X-15, and similar air brakes subsequently appeared on the Space Shuttle. Some tests were carried out with an X-shaped tail section to try and avoid airflow interference from the wing, rather than mounting the horizontal tail high on the fin or low on the fuselage like other contemporary supersonic designs. In the end, it was found that placing the horizontal stabilizer in the same plane as the wing avoided this interference and allowed for the construction of a conventional empennage.

Just released from its EB-50 in 1956, the X-2 begins one of its last series of flights. Its pilot, Korean War ace Capt Iven Kincheloe, was selected as USAF project pilot on the X-15 in 1958, but he lost his life in an F-104 accident in July of that year. On September 7, 1956 he had reached a record 126,200ft in the X-2, thus becoming the "first man in space." His attitude to the danger of test flying was simple – "I got into it because I wanted to. If I didn't, 15 other guys were waiting to do it." (NASA)

In 1954 the availability of suitable rocket engines remained problematic, and the General Electric A1 Hermes, a missile engine, was an early but ultimately unsuitable candidate. It seemed that the only option was several relatively low-powered units in combinations to vary the overall thrust in lieu of throttle control. Two more years elapsed before design work was commissioned on a throttleable engine specifically for the X-15.

Despite the formidable technological challenges still ahead, Becker felt sufficiently confident in the project by May 1954 to invite a conference of NACA, USAF and (as something of an afterthought) US Navy representatives to hear his proposals. There was already a sense of urgency and a determination to build such a revolutionary machine within only three years. The meeting took place on July 9, and Hugh Dryden, an early proponent of high-speed flight, asserted NACA's support for the hypersonic project. He was advised to seek Department of Defense (DoD) approval and assured that the delegates would study the provisions of the NACA Langley design proposals.

The US Navy delegation surprised the gathering by revealing that the Douglas Aircraft Company had already been contracted to study a follow-up to the D-558-II Skyrocket – the air-launched Model 671 that would fly to an altitude of 1,000,000ft at Mach 7. Resembling the D-558-II with larger tail surfaces, it had a single 50,000lb-thrust rocket engine and a ventral fin that could be jettisoned before landing. Douglas suggested highly innovative ways of dispersing frictional heat including a titanium main structure with a temporary ablative coating over the external skin. The leading edges of the flying surfaces, where the highest temperatures of up to 3,300 degrees F would occur, were to be either sprayed with water to create heat-removing steam or protected by chilled oxygen pumped into the boundary-layer airstream. Thruster jets in the tail and wingtips powered by steam generated by catalyzed hydrogen peroxide would give high-altitude directional control. The designers chose an ejectable nose section, like the Bell X-2's.

Interestingly, pressure suits for the pilot were dismissed partly because suit pressurization could not be maintained during ejection. The team saw that a new type of sensor would be needed to measure pitch and yaw or sideslip at high altitudes where conventional methods would not work. Douglas engineers had considered many of the problems that would also face the X-15 and devised a number of interesting solutions, some of which were echoed in the X-15 design.

Although the Model 671 was rejected and the US Navy's role in the X-15 project remained a token one, the study generated useful ideas, and the July 9 meeting brought a real focus on the hypersonic initiative. The USAF's Wright Air Development Center (WADC) at Dayton, Ohio, evaluated the Langley proposal by August 13, 1954, estimating that it would take at least four years and $12.2m to implement. By September there was general agreement on the need for hypersonic research as a single, joint project (unlike the Model 671), and on the need for a manned aircraft with performance significantly superior to current military aircraft projects. A month later WADC endorsed the Langley proposals to USAF Headquarters, emphasizing that the new aircraft should be seen as a pure research vehicle with no operational potential. "Sole executive responsibility" would rest with the USAF, but the aircraft would be passed to NACA after initial USAF acceptance trials.

At a meeting of NACA's Committee on Aerodynamics on October 4 Walter Williams won almost unanimous support for the project. The only objection came from Kelly Johnson, designer of many of Lockheed's exceptionally innovative aircraft, who had found the performance of previous X-planes disappointing and argued that all new projects should be prototypes for production military aircraft.

At a further meeting on October 22, Soulé discussed detailed specifications for the new design with WADC specialists. Becker's study was the main focus, although the US Navy, which would have a ten percent share in funding the project in return for very little active participation, had already requested a second "observer's" seat in the aircraft. WADC suggested three aircraft, with NACA having technical direction of the project. Due largely to Hugh Dryden's influence, the Memorandum of Understanding produced on October 22 strongly recommended the hypersonic aircraft as "a matter of national urgency." Further project refinement continued until December 1954, when the DoD's Air Technical Advisory Panel approved the project. On December 30 the USAF invited 12 manufacturers to tender for the hypersonic contract, which on January 17, 1955 became Project 1226, System 447L or the X-15.

This wide selection took into account the lack of commercial profit from such a small batch of highly sophisticated aircraft that would require enormous research and risk with no prospect of extended production. Even the valuable data the aircraft generated was to be made available by NACA free of charge. Most of the companies also lacked any relevant experience when it came to building aircraft of this type. Weighing this liability against potential benefits in publicity and manufacturing experience took three firms – Grumman, Martin and (unsurprisingly) Lockheed – out of the competition. However, senior figures from Douglas, Bell, Boeing, and Northrop attended the bidders' conference, where each company provided one main design and an alternative proposal.

The basic specification was for an aircraft capable of a speed of 6,600ft/sec and an altitude of 250,000ft carrying 800lb of research instrumentation in a 40cu ft compartment. The first aircraft was to be ready within 30 months of contract signature.

By the May 9, 1955 deadline only four companies had submitted ideas. With Boeing, Chance-Vought, McDonnell, Convair and Northrop having also withdrawn, Douglas and Bell seemed the best-qualified contenders – both had proven track records in rocket-powered X-plane development. North American Aviation and Republic also remained in the competition. Meanwhile, NACA established an evaluation committee (which included Williams, Becker and Soulé) for the submissions. The USAF appointed Capt Chester E. McCollough as WADC project engineer and handed their management of the project to WADC's Fighter Aircraft Division. George A. Spangenberg became the US Navy's project engineer. Evaluation was to be a complex, three-month process involving the specialist divisions of NACA (which became the National Aeronautics and Space Administration (NASA) after September 1958).

THE CONTENDERS

Bell had built the X-1 and X-2, and it produced rocket engines, so it seemed a strong potential X-15 contender. Its D-171 proposal used three Bell XLR-81 motors, each of which produced 14,500lb thrust but also allowed an 8,000lb "half-thrust" setting so that combinations of the three motors could vary the overall power. The motor was under development to power the B-58A Hustler bomber's nuclear weapon pod.

Like the other final proposals, the D-171 echoed both the original Becker outline and dimensions and those of the X-2. Two fully retractable landing skids were located under the center section, with a wheeled nose-gear and relatively conventional wing and tail-unit layouts. The D-171 had a drag-reducing flush canopy like the X-1, but it also had the disadvantage of hazardous red fuming nitric oxide as the oxidizer for the XLR-81's fuel system. Bell preferred this to a liquid oxygen (lox) oxidizer partly because it would not require a complex topping-off system in its carrier aircraft to keep the lox tanks full. However, the nitric acid required considerable storage space in two large fuselage tanks. A reaction control system using eight small hydrogen peroxide thrusters was included for high-altitude flying control.

Rejecting a full Inconel-X structure, Bell designers opted for a "double wall" panel method some 3,000lb lighter by using a thinner Inconel-X outer skin welded to a corrugated Inconel-X inner skin, with an air gap to provide insulation. Each small panel was able to expand under severe heating, sliding under a retaining strip that covered each panel joint. Rather than employing the well-established EB-50 carrier aircraft, Bell chose the giant Convair B-36 Peacemaker bomber to perform this

important role instead, the latter having already been adapted to carry an RF-84K fighter in Project FICON (FIghter CONveyer). A two-seat version was also drafted in accordance with the US Navy requirement. Bell considered the 30-month deadline impossible to meet, however, anticipating that 46 months would be needed before the first glide flight could be made.

Douglas followed its earlier Skyrocket design precedents for its Model 684 submission to some extent, but used a straight wing made from relatively thick half-inch magnesium/thorium-zirconium alloy (HK31) with copper leading edges. Douglas judged that magnesium would be lighter and easier to machine than Inconel-X, having used similar metal in its previous rocket-planes. It was acknowledged that the alloy would not re-radiate heat as effectively as Inconel-X, but in brief exposures to extreme heat this was considered tolerable.

Douglas used a similar escape system to the Skyrocket's, with a jettisonable, parachute-equipped forward fuselage. There was a small cockpit canopy that gave better visibility than the flush versions of the Bell and Republic designs, and the aircraft was unique among the submissions in having a conventional wheeled undercarriage with a supplementary tailwheel in its wedge-shaped ventral stabilizer. Its rocket powerplant was a single Reaction Motors XLR-30 "Super Viking," a development of the XLR-10 used in the US Navy's Viking research rocket and the favored motor for the X-15 program with its lox and ammonia propellant combination. The Model 684 would have been light enough to use an EB-50 carrier aircraft.

ABOVE LEFT
Rocket-powered flight inevitably involved hazardous substances, in this case hydrogen peroxide for the X-15's reaction control system. The X-15's propellant tanks each had a cylindrical core holding helium for pressurizing the tanks and three connected chambers for the lox and ammonia, each one a potential bomb. The X-15 program used prodigious quantities of propellants. The totals for 1961 alone included 246,000 gallons of ammonia, 60,000 gallons of alcohol, 3,500 tons of nitrogen and 420,000lb of peroxide. Ground testing used a substantial proportion. The smell of ammonia was a constant presence for those working around the X-15 and, like the hydrogen peroxide, it was far more concentrated than the domestic versions. (NASA)

Republic Aviation offered a much heavier proposal, the AP-76, which drew upon the company's design experience with the XF-91 jet/rocket fighter (boosted by an XLR-11 rocket, the XF-91 was the first combat aircraft prototype to fly supersonic in level flight) and the projected Mach 3.7 XF-103 interceptor, powered by a combined turbojet-and-ramjet Wright XJ-67 engine. Its AP-76 required four of the XLR-81 engines also chosen by Bell, yielding 58,000lb total thrust from its hypergolic (igniting spontaneously on contact) propellants – red fuming nitric oxide and a mixture of kerosene and dimethylhydrazine. A complex arrangement of nine switches was used to select various engine combinations to vary the power.

Although the AP-76's overall configuration was similar to the other contenders, its nose section, like the XF-103's, had no cockpit canopy, giving low drag and frictional heating but visibility that was restricted to small side windows panels. A mirror system that peeped out through a hatch above the cockpit gave limited forward vision at low speed.

Republic preferred a newly devised sandwich of titanium with a corrugated Inconel-X outer skin, separated by blocks of Marinite insulation. Titanium carbide alloy was prescribed for the flying surface leading edges. The aircraft was unique in having a three-skid undercarriage, and it had reaction control thrusters linked to the main control column – a system later explored by NAA. Finally, it needed the B-36H carrier aircraft to take it aloft. Republic's back-up proposal involved a 29in fuselage extension for a second cockpit but, unlike the other designs, it retained space for scientific instruments.

By June 10, 1955 the evaluators put the NAA proposal narrowly ahead of the Douglas Model 684. Bell was a surprising third and the weighty, complex Republic submission last. NAA had never built a rocket-plane but it had substantial missile experience beginning with captured V2s and leading to the 1950s' Mach 3 Navaho long-range cruise missile. The company was also involved in very advanced research for the innovative Mach 3 XB-70 bomber, and it had a long and distinguished record of building vital USAF combat aircraft, notably the P-51 Mustang, F-86 Sabre and F-100 Super Sabre.

NAA's Advanced Design Group, led by Hugh Elkin, welcomed another challenge and originated a design based closely on the Langley specifications. Concentrating on the "art of the possible" and relatively simple solutions rather more than the other teams, they consulted extensively with Edwards AFB personnel.

Inconel-X, in taper-milled skin panels, was approved as the principal structural material to resist temperatures between 800 and 1,200 degrees F. However, extreme heating on leading-edge areas was absorbed by replaceable leading-edge sections using materials such as laminated glass cloth that could burn or melt – an idea that Langley rejected. Making the lox and anhydrous ammonia propellant tanks integral with the semi-monocoque central fuselage saved weight. Two large "tunnel" fairings were added to the fuselage sides to accommodate control cables, propellant plumbing and wiring looms. Like the Douglas design, it used wedge-shaped upper and lower vertical stabilizers and the Reaction Motors XLR-30 engine. The landing gear consisted of rear skids and a twin nose-wheel unit, and a fighter-type cockpit canopy was provided. A B-36H would launch the aircraft at around 38,000ft and Mach 0.6.

The selection of NAA's design reflected NACA's belief that it could surpass the basic requirements while complying with the aims of the NACA project. There were doubts about the landing gear and the horizontal stabilizer, with 15 degrees of anhedral, which was intended to work as a single unit for pitch control and as two individual surfaces for roll control (the "rolling tail"), instead of using separate ailerons and elevators. No objections were raised over the major cost increases that most firms had factored in – NAA wanted $20.1m more than the lowest estimate by Bell of $36.3m, and X-plane history suggested that these figures would inevitably increase significantly. The US Navy, despite historically favoring Douglas, went along with NACA and the USAF when the evaluation verdict was delivered in the first week of August 1955. The recommendation of NAA, with a proposed development schedule extension, went to the Assistant Secretary of Defense for Research and Development after a final meeting on August 12.

Only 11 days later NAA verbally informed Capt McCollough that the firm did not want to proceed with the project. Faced with the prospect of having to resort to an expensively re-engineered version of the Douglas Model 684, with Inconel-X rather than magnesium alloy structure, Hugh Dryden announced that he was proceeding with the NAA procurement procedure and would prefer to re-start the competition if NAA definitely withdrew. In fact, an 18-month stretch in the schedule persuaded NAA's president, John "Lee" Atwood, to reconsider the program.

He had been concerned that his designers were already fully committed to the XB-70 bomber and Mach 3 F-108 Rapier interceptor – the two most important USAF combat aircraft programs of the time – although both lacked production contracts. NAA was also developing its F-107, an advanced update of the F-100 Super Sabre, although the USAF chose the Republic F-105 instead. The letter of withdrawal was retracted in September 1955 and an official contract for three aircraft, B-36 modifications, and initial testing was drawn up by June 11, 1956. Reaction Motors also signed a contract for the government-funded Project 3116 to provide a rocket motor for the NAA design.

Raymond Rice, NAA's vice-president, who had initially rejected the contract for this small, risky, low-profit venture, delegated the role of chief designer for Project 1226 to Harrison A. Storms, who was told by Rice that "we could have the program on condition that none of the problems were ever to be brought into his office – it would be up to me to seek all the solutions." Fortunately, whereas others at NAA had seen the X-15 mainly as a theoretical design exercise, Storms believed in the project and willingly accepted charge of one of the world's most complex and technologically challenging aircraft.

CHAPTER TWO

BUILDING THE BLACK BEAST

X-15-1 on the pylon of NB52A 52003 at the end of its first captive flight (1-C-1) on March 10, 1959. Scott Crossfield, glimpsed in the cockpit, checks the X-15's undercarriage extension while "Balls 3," flown by Messrs Bock, Allavie and Berkowitz, has its forward undercarriage truck lowered onto the runway. Charles Feltz was determined that the aircraft should remain within its weight limits and not be overloaded with scientific research packages. Despite its space-age appearance, the X-15 was mainly designed with slide rules, pens and paper in the absence of adequate computers. (Boeing)

Harrison Storms received more useful advice from Hartley Soulé, who explained that "You have a little airplane and a big engine with a large thrust margin. We want to go to an altitude of 250,000ft and reach Mach 6. We want to study aerodynamic heating. We don't want to worry about aerodynamic stability and control, or the airplane breaking up. So if you make errors, make them on the strong side." The aircraft had to be designed to cope with forces of +4g and -2g under power, increasing to +7.33 g and -3g during its re-entry to the atmosphere from 250,000ft at almost 4,300mph.

Storms quickly assembled a 35-man team, with 39-year-old Texan Charles Feltz (a veteran of the F-86 Sabre program) as chief project engineer. Working 15-hour days, he would manage the team's daily business with outstanding success. Walter Williams at NACA maintained close links and supplied wind-tunnel test data on X-15 models. Some information on hypersonics was available, which meant that the X-15 would not be leaping completely into the unknown, as Bell's X-1 had done. Later wind-tunnel installations at NACA Ames (using captured German components) and the Gas Dynamics Laboratory increased test-conditions airspeeds to Mach 12 by 1958, mainly for research into ICBMs. Whereas the relatively gradual programs for the Bell and Douglas rocket-planes kept their speed just ahead of what production military jets were achieving, the X-15 would

Albert Scott Crossfield

Born in California with Irish, English and Hispanic origins, Scott Crossfield was brought up with a strong work ethic and became a self-confessed perfectionist. Surviving near-fatal pneumonia as a child (at one point he was given the last rites), he became obsessed with flying. Crossfield idolized test pilots, and he made his first solo flight while still at school, attempting to build his own aircraft at the age of 17. After training as an engineer from 1940 and spending nine months working at Boeing, he joined the US Navy in 1942, becoming an instructor and an aerobatic team leader.

Postwar, Crossfield returned to studying, receiving a master's degree in aeronautical science in 1950 and then joined NACA's High-Speed Flight Station. He flew many of the early X-planes, including the X-1 and the D-558 series; at the controls of the latter aircraft, he became the first pilot to reach Mach 2 in November 1953. While at NASA Crossfield's Boeing experience and aeronautical science knowledge impelled him to apply to Bell during its X-2 project, hoping to improve the efficiency and costings of what he saw as a failing project. At that stage he was kept at Edwards AFB, but when the X-15 project began he moved to NAA in 1955 and became closely involved in its design and manufacturing as well as making the initial flights. He told Walter Williams that he wanted to fly the X-15, "but I want to help build it too. I want to be a part of that airplane," and he thought that he could have more influence over it from within NAA than from a distance at NACA. At NAA until 1967, Crossfield worked on the Hound Dog missile, Apollo command and service module, and Saturn booster as Technical Director, Research Engineering and Test.

Among the many awards he received were the Collier and Harmon trophies, Sperry, Octave Chanute and Kincheloe awards and induction into the National Aviation Hall of Fame, International Space Hall of Fame and Aerospace Walk of Honor. Crossfield perished on April 19, 2006 when

X-plane test pilot Scott Crossfield became a major influence on the X-15 project. He lived in Los Angeles and flew to work in his own Beechcraft Bonanza, becoming so involved with the early development of the X-15 that colleague "Pete" Knight said Crossfield "felt it was his airplane." (Bell Aircraft)

his Cessna 210A aircraft broke up near Montgomery, Alabama, in unexpectedly stormy weather.

leap ahead in virtually every respect, validating existing wind-tunnel results as well as supplying new data.

Experienced test pilot Scott Crossfield had joined Walt Williams in presenting the first operational specifications for the X-15 on October 4, 1954. At NAA as a consultant, Crossfield quickly became closely involved in the design process as, in his own estimation, "the X-15's chief son-of-a-bitch. Anyone who wanted Charles Feltz or North American to capriciously change anything or add anything would first have to fight me." Although his somewhat egocentric personality alienated many, his practical input to the development of the new aircraft was considerable. Crossfield insisted on a full-pressure suit for its pilot, and he was instrumental in evolving one with the David Clark

Company. He also strongly recommended an ejection seat rather than the USAF-sponsored capsule system.

As the design firmed up there were many challenges. Although the basic layout was quite conventional, the airframe was unique in its use of innovative metals with largely untried qualities. Uncertainties concerning the choice of structural materials prompted further research into ceramic-metallic, fiberglass and titanium carbide, as well as the inclusion of removable wing leading edges in order to try different materials. NACA was also worried that vortices from the fuselage side-tunnels would disturb airflow over the vertical stabilizers. The "side-tunnel" fairings, an innovation by design team member George Owl, helped to restore performance that had been reduced by weight increases. They created about half of the aircraft's lift at high speed.

In order to tolerate the high-g conditions of its unexplored flight profiles, the airframe had to be sufficiently strong and stiff for potential overload factors. The outer skin of heat-treated Inconel-X covered a structure using titanium for some sections of the fuselage and wings, apart from the inner pressure shell of the cockpit and instrumentation bay which used high-strength aluminum (2024-T). One of the titanium alloys used (6A1-4V) could be welded using fusion or resistance techniques but, as Lockheed found in using titanium for its A-12 and SR-71, it was difficult to work and it required innovative manufacturing techniques, as did Huntington Alloys' Inconel-X, which posed numerous welding problems. Harrison Storms noted that, lacking any information on assembly method using Inconel-X, "The development had to be done by North American in forming, welding and otherwise joining this material." After 1956 it replaced some of the titanium carbide alloy intended as heat-sink material in the wing and tail surfaces.

Even the cockpit transparencies required a new material since triple-layer panes of soda-lime-tempered glass would only withstand 750 degrees F rather than the anticipated 1,000 degrees F, with temperature differentials of 750 degrees F between the panes. The Corning Glass Company developed outer panes of alumina-silicate glass that could survive 1,500 degrees F. An early strengthening addition was a pressurization system for the propellant tanks to give them extra rigidity when emptied. Fuselage diameter was slightly increased and the tanks were lengthened to take an extra 2,500lb of fuel, adding 0.5 Mach to the potential top speed.

POWER

Among the four possible X-15 rocket motors listed by the USAF's Power Plant Laboratory, NAA offered its own experimental NA 5400 giving only 5,400lb of thrust. Aerojet's XLR-73, producing 10,000lb of thrust, was not favored as the X-15 would have

The XLR-99 throttle control on the left of the cockpit allowed thrust settings of between 50 and 100 percent. The motor was designed to offer lower power settings, but the XLR-99 usually cut out if it was set below 50 percent. After two failed re-light attempts ejection was recommended. Normal burn-out was after about 80 seconds. The 7ft-long motor weighed 910lb and its nozzle was 24in in diameter. Its compact structure made it hard to service. Only eight of these incredibly loud motors were used by the X-15 flight program. (AFFTC/Landis)

needed four or more. The Bell XLR-81BA1 promised 15,000lb of thrust from a mixture of unsymmetrical dimethylhydrazine and jet fuel ("JPX"), but it could not be re-started – a requirement for X-15 operations.

Reaction Motors Inc (RMI) had a proven record in producing aircraft rocket motors, and its planned XLR-30, using a similar, weight-saving "regenerative cooling" system to its earlier XLR-11 and chosen by Douglas and, eventually, by NAA under USAF pressure, was the most promising contender. Developed from the XLR-10 for the US Navy's Viking rocket, it used cooling tubes to circulate the cold propellants around the motor before they entered the combustion chambers. It also introduced a "bleed turbine" mechanism that used a mixture of fuel and gases from the combustion section to propel the fuel system circulation turbine.

The result was a single, compact powerplant with almost nine times the XLR-11's thrust but around 100lb less weight. However, RMI still had to develop a throttleable version of the engine, which was under development primarily for naval ballistic missiles. They assured the bid selectors that they could provide variable power between 17,000lb (30 percent thrust) and 57,000lb thrust and enable the engine to make at least five in-flight re-starts, unlike any previous rocket motor. However, the XLR-30 was not ready, and it was clear by July 1957 that there would be a nine-month gap between the airframe and engine development schedules.

There was some concern expressed from NACA's Lewis laboratory about using highly corrosive ammonia as a propellant and it was suggested that it could be replaced by JP4 jet fuel. Both promised similar performance, but the cost of delaying for a switch to JP4 ruled it out. The motor's ability to re-start repeatedly was also questioned.

Even before X-15 contracts were signed Williams foresaw that an interim power source, probably several XLR-11s, would be required for the early proving flights. However, RMI received a contract on October 26, 1955, and by February 1956 it had submitted a detailed proposal including a 30-month development period and a designation – XLR-99-RM-1.

At RMI Harry Koch, Wesley Schilling and Robert Seaman were tasked with developing the complex new engine which had to be throttleable, deliver 57,000lb of thrust (in fact the thrust varied, and it could develop up to 60,000lb at an altitude of 100,000ft), weigh 618lb and burn for 90 seconds at maximum power. The estimated cost in 1955 was $6m (although this figure had increased sevenfold by mid-1959) for ten engines. When a $450,000 rocket test facility was opened at Edwards AFB in June 1959, primarily for the XLR-99, the engine was still a year away from using it. Two non-flying X-15 aft fuselages were constructed for RMI to use in developing the engine installation.

The motor gradually matured into a safe, reliable powerplant, but only after numerous problems had been solved. The most challenging of these included overcoming engine vibration, rectifying fuel pump

An XLR-99 installed in the first X-15, which is suspended on its NB-52 pylon. The bomber's inboard flap area was notched to accept the X-15's vertical stabilizer. Developed in a program managed by Harry Cook, the XLR-99 was the key to the X-15 hypersonic flights. Although it developed unprecedented power and proved generally reliable, the motor's throttling process (controlled by varying the turbo-pump speed) was sensitive and caused many unintended shut-downs. Milt Thompson's May 21, 1964 flight was curtailed by the pilot's inability to restart the engine due to a pressure "spike" in the engine's second-stage pressure-sensing line. He had accelerated to Mach 2.9 but had to make the program's first diversion to Cuddeback Dry Lake, landing so fast and so far down the lake that he crossed a road at 100mph, cutting through the banks on each side of it and ploughing on for another 500ft. Remarkably, there was no serious damage to pilot or plane. (NASA)

Crossfield rides X-15-1 beneath NB-52A 52-003 while Bob Baker and cameraman John DeLong, both from NAA, keep pace in Chase One, a company support F-100F (59-3963). This October 31, 1959 mission turned into a weather abort. Pilot Milt Thompson commented that the uncomfortable 4g acceleration made the X-15 the only plane he flew where he was "glad when the engine quit." With the XLR-99, the aircraft could accelerate from Mach 5 to Mach 6 in six seconds. As Bob White commented, "You flipped the switch and held on." Acceleration kept the pilot firmly pushed against the back of his seat throughout powered flight. (AFFTC)

leaks and working out how to prevent the Rokide protective ceramic coating that lined the firing chamber from peeling off.

By July 1958 numerous refinements to the basic X-15 design had been requested following the mock-up inspection in December 1956. To improve longitudinal stability the side-tunnel fairings were cut back ahead of the wing, the horizontal stabilizer was moved back 5.4in and the vertical stabilizer's area was increased, making the dorsal and ventral areas roughly symmetrical. The speed brakes were made smaller in size to reduce risk of flutter and the vertical surfaces became adjustable to allow for asymmetrical thrust from the rocket motor. Throughout this process constant balancing of increases and savings in weight continued. At the end of 1955 the team's efforts to keep the overall weight within limits were undermined by new research figures which showed that the amount of heat-absorbing structure, particularly in the lower fuselage, would be inadequate. NAA had to add another 2,000lb of metalwork to soak up anticipated heat, although during flight testing it was found that these temperature estimates were actually several hundred degrees too high.

BOOSTER BOMBER

Although the earliest rocket-planes could take off from the ground, it was clear that their few minutes of powered flight made high-altitude launch from a carrier aircraft a more practical alternative. B-29 and B-50 bombers had been used to haul the first X-planes aloft, but the X-15 needed a more powerful carrier to launch it higher and faster. The gigantic B-36H with a wingspan of 230ft was Strategic Air Command's primary heavy bomber from 1949, and it could have reached 50,000ft at over 400mph with an X-15 and its support crew and equipment semi-recessed into its massive bomb-bay. Preparations were made in 1956 to modify a B-36 for the X-15 program, with flight testing from October 1958. The bomber would have been tilted upwards with ramps beneath its main undercarriage and the X-15 towed beneath

X-15-1 rolling slightly to the right as it leaves the pylon, influenced by down-wash from the NB-52A's wing and the airflow along its fuselage. Normally, as the X-15 fell away the NB-52 would go slightly nose-up and bank left, requiring some re-trimming. Assisted flight for rocket-planes originated in 1941 in Germany when the Me 163A V4 was towed to 13,500ft to begin its record-breaking, but secret, 623mph flight. (Boeing)

the bomb-bay and then winched up into the B-36 and suspended from three points on the rocket-plane's upper fuselage.

By 1957 the X-15 Joint Operations Committee had begun to explore other carrier options to the soon-to-be-obsolete B-36, seeking higher launch speeds to compensate for potential weight increases as the X-15 evolved. Convair's supersonic B-58A Hustler was evaluated, but there was insufficient space between its landing gear units and podded engines to allow for an X-15, even if the latter's vertical tail folded down. Boeing's KC-135 tanker was also briefly considered, but its low-mounted wing and short, fuselage-housed main undercarriage also left no room for an X-15.

The company's B-52 bomber presented similar undercarriage limitations which ruled out bomb-bay carriage. However, its high-mounted wing and generous space between the fuselage and inboard engine nacelle gave room for a large support pylon, and Boeing had already decided to use this facility for pylon-mounted GAM-77 Hound Dog missiles. The wing could support a 50,000lb load at that point, so a relatively bulky pylon could be installed to support the X-15 and its pilot, who would obviously have to enter the rocket-plane's cockpit on the ground and remain in place as the duo ascended for around 90 minutes to launch altitude. However, the considerable advantages in launch speed and altitude outweighed lack of access to the X-15 in flight.

Two B-52 prototypes (an XB-52 and a YB-52) were initially offered, but X-15 program managers were concerned about spares and maintenance problems with these non-standard models. The USAF requisitioned an early production B-52A (52-003) in October 1957 instead, and added an early RB-52B (52-008) in May 1958, both from Boeing's test fleet. The first, modified as NB-52A *The High and Mighty One*, was delivered to Edwards AFB on November 14, 1958, followed by NB-52B 52008 *The Challenger* (more commonly known as "Balls 8") on June 8, 1959.

The distinctive steering controllers on each side-console, in addition to the central "stick," distinguish the X-15 cockpit from conventional types. The central Attitude Indicator (white and black) showed the aircraft's position relative to the horizon and indicated side-slip, but a later modification to it contributed to the program's only fatal accident. Many of the dials displayed pressure, temperature, and status of the various fuel substances. Most pilots found the right side-stick controller easier to use than the center-stick when their pressure suits were inflated. (North American Aviation)

Structural changes included the removal of a fuel cell from the right wing, inactivation of the inboard flaps and the stripping out of all military systems. A pylon containing hydraulic release gear for the X-15 plus a pneumatic back-up system was located under the right wing. A cut-out in the right inboard flap provided clearance for the rocket-plane's vertical tail. The NB-52s were equipped with AN/APN-81 Doppler radar systems to feed the X-15's all-new stable platform, and upgraded UHF communication equipment was also installed. They also supplied the rocket-plane's electrical power, oxygen for the pilot and radio communications.

Two TV cameras, floodlights and three 16mm cine cameras were installed in the right fuselage side, and the launch operator (seated in the former electronic countermeasures operator's compartment) monitored the launch and topping-off of the X-15's lox tanks through the cameras. An astrodome-type transparency was also subsequently added. Two of the B-52's fuselage fuel cells were removed to accommodate two liquid oxygen tanks, holding 1,500 gallons in all, and 24 cylinders for storage of nitrogen and helium for the X-15's systems. "Topping off" the X-15's lox supply as it boiled off during the pre-launch ascent required 600 to 800 gallons.

The reduction in the B-52's flap area increased its normal landing speed of 174 knots, requiring new high-speed wheels and brakes rated to 218 knots and some new "no-flaps" takeoff and landing techniques, developed by NB-52 pilots Capts Charles C. Bock and John E. "Jack" Allavie, who were allocated to the program together with X-15 launch panel operator Bill Berkovitz from NAA. The B-52 normally lifted off and landed with all four of its landing gear "trucks" leaving or meeting the ground almost at once, but the two pilots realized that they would have to rotate the bomber around its rear landing gear to develop enough lift without the aid of flaps. A trim setting of two degrees, nose-up, made the big bomber rotate within an acceptable distance, but the pilots also had to develop techniques for landing on the rear undercarriage units, deploying the drag 'chute and air brakes as soon as the forward landing gear made contact too. The drag 'chute was crucial, particularly when landing with the X-15 still attached.

Wind-tunnel and ground tests indicated that the NB-52/X-15 combination would be trouble-free, although there were some concerns about the rocket-plane's tail being so close to the noisy jet efflux from the NB-52's No. 5 engine. To avoid potential detriment to the fatigue life of parts of the X-15 airframe through prolonged exposure to more than 160 decibels, NAA decided to reinforce the structure of the vertical and horizontal stabilizers with larger rivets, heavier-duty ribs and dimpled skin.

PILOTING

By November 1955 the arrangement of the pilot's flying controls had been decided. A central control column operated the conventional control surfaces, with an alternative, linked, side-stick controller on the right side-console. Another side-stick controller on the left side-console opened the small hydrogen-peroxide jets of the reaction control system for high-altitude flight. The side-stick idea, favored by Crossfield, was tested (like the stable platform) on the YF-107A fighter, where it was found that pilots tended to over-control due to the stick's short travel. It could be finely adjusted through five fore-and-aft locations to suit the pilot's arm length. These controls linked easily to the "rolling tail," and pilots found few differences in handling compared with conventional ailerons and horizontal stabilizers.

X-15-1 in December 1960 with the eight XLR-11 tubes visible and evidence that the jettisonable lower ventral rudder has been parachuted safely for reuse ten times. The ventral rudder parachute recovery system had been tested on JF-104A 55-2961. (Landis Collection)

When launching from a carrier aircraft or preparing for re-entry, the pilot would carefully check his horizontal stabilizer setting on the position indicator. The two sections of the rudder were operated by conventional pedals, and the lower ventral fin and rudder were jettisoned with a parachute just before landing to give adequate ground clearance. The ventral fin gave stability at subsonic speeds and moderate angles of attack and the rear section of the fixed ventral portion opened out to form a pair of air brakes linked to a pair in the dorsal fin area. Four extending speed-brake segments were deployed towards the end of the final approach when the pilot had enough runway in sight, enabling more accurate landings. They also controlled the astonishing rate of climb.

Aerodynamic controls were intended for use up to an altitude of 180,000ft, at which point the ballistic control system with its hydrogen-peroxide, steam-emitting thrusters took over. There were eight

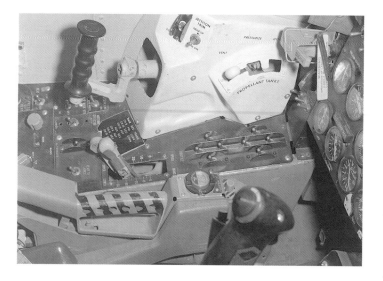

The left side cockpit console of the X-15-1 fitted with XLR-11 motors. The left (ballistic) side controller dominated a console that also housed the trim control switch, engine throttle, flap, propellant jettison, and speed brake controls, together with controls for the SAS, reaction control system, and UHF radio and the eight separate switches for the XLR-11 rocket chambers (just below the propellant tanks control). These were later replaced by a single throttle lever for the XLR-99. Operating the X-15's controls while wearing a full-pressure suit required many hours of practice. (NASA Dryden)

thrusters, each with a 1.40in vent, in the nose, with pairs pointing left, right, up and down for pitch and yaw, and emitting 113lb of thrust. There were two in each wingtip, generating 40lb thrust each, pointing up and down for roll control to keep the wings level. They usually consumed only two gallons of peroxide per flight. Above 170,000ft, thrusters were the only way to control the aircraft's attitude and prevent it from flying sideways or even backwards as it approached re-entry to the atmosphere.

It was important to focus on establishing stability in one axis (either roll or pitch and yaw) at a time or the pilot could easily become disorientated. In practice, pilots would use the thrusters to emit "blips" of steam in addition to the conventional controls at around 100,000ft, although they were not very precise.

The first X-15 at the end of a test flight after installation of the "ball nose." Although it was generally successful, the Northrop-developed "ball" system was unable to detect any airflow above 230,000ft, meaning that AoA had to be calculated by NASA-1 from the ground. Post-flight, it was protected by a fiberglass shell. Also visible are the nose-mounted reaction control nozzles. This system was initially plagued by leaky control valves and frozen steam nozzles, delaying its use in the second and third aircraft. Pilots could hear when the nose thrusters fired and feel the associated vibration. (AFFTC)

Overall stability was maintained by a Westinghouse stability augmentation system (SAS) operating in all three axes (pitch, roll and yaw) via rate gyros, servo-cylinders and dampers. SAS was essential for control at angles of attack (AoA) greater than ten degrees, but failures became quite common during the flight program, although most occurred during ground tests. The aircraft's handling characteristics were very similar to those predicted by simulations at NASA Ames laboratories.

Also for use at high altitudes, where normal pitot-tube sensors would not work, was the innovative "ball nose" at the tip of the aircraft's nose to measure AoA and sideslip angle. It was also known as the "Q-ball" because it measured dynamic pressure, or "Q." Northrop's Nortronics Division used a basic NASA design to produce six "Q-ball" units for use in the X-15, comprising a 6.5in-diameter spherical sensor at the tip of the aircraft's nose, with 70lb of related electronic, hydraulic and pneumatic equipment housed behind it. Cooled by nitrogen, the "ball" was hydraulically rotated in a steel collar mount so that it always faced into the airstream. Through pressure-sensing orifices it could detect angles of attack from -10 degrees to +40 degrees and sideslip angles of ±20 degrees. Its Inconel-X skin resisted sustained temperatures of 1,200 degrees F, although one unit was tested to more than 2,400 degrees F in the afterburner of a Super Sabre, emerging with only minor damage.

When a revised unit was needed for the greater Mach 8 aerodynamic heating to be faced by the later X-15A-2 version, NASA developed TAZ-8A ceramic/metal alloy for the "ball," tested in the afterburner of a Lockheed F-104's J79 turbojet. While development of the "Q-ball" was still awaiting completion, a normal 71in NACA air data boom was fitted for the initial low-speed portion of the flight test program.

The other major innovation in flying control was the stable platform – a device to measure the aircraft's performance and location during flight. A new system, which pre-dated the inertial navigation systems (INS) of the 1960s, it initially operated as an analog system using early solid-state electronics. Although at first unreliable, a revised Honeywell digital version, based on the system for the canceled X-20 (Dyna-Soar) was installed in two X-15s from 1964–65. It used an Inertial Flight Data System that measured altitude, climb rate, velocity and attitude. Information to align the platform came from the NB-52 carrier aircraft's AN/APN-81 Doppler radar and N-1 gyro-stabilized magnetic compass.

The 176lb unit, produced by the Sperry Gyroscope Company, used a four-gimbal platform, and information appeared on cockpit displays showing pitch, roll and heading on an "eight-ball" rotating spherical display that included a small aircraft picture, positioned in relation to the ground, horizon and sky. The nitrogen-cooled stable platform was available after the X-15 completed its initial trials, for which it was unnecessary. The platform was aligned just prior to launch, and it then presented data on velocity and height for five minutes and continued to offer pitch, roll and drift/yaw information for 20 minutes. Compared with later ring-laser gyro systems, it lacked accuracy and reliability. However, the revised Honeywell inertial flight data system could align itself without data inputs from the NB-52, and its digital computer proved more dependable. Reliability improved considerably during 1965, and it remained in the second X-15 after its conversion to an X-15A-2.

Together with hundreds of telemetry pickups, load sensors, thermocouples and strain gauges throughout the airframe, the X-15 carried more instrumentation than any previous aircraft. Even this sophisticated equipment did not rule out the vital necessity of a stop-watch in the cockpit.

ESCAPE

While the X-15 was being conceived, the USAF decided that all new high-performance aircraft should have an escape capsule for high-speed ejections where the human body was likely to be subjected to intolerable forces. The B-58A Hustler was re-equipped with encapsulated seats devised in 1958 and the General Dynamics F-111 was designed with an ejectable cockpit section. Similar seats were contemplated for some single-seat fighters but their weight and complexity deterred further development.

For the X-15 a capsule system could have added up to 9,000lb, effectively negating all the weight-saving targets that Charles Feltz had established. Crossfield was adamant that escape capsules were potentially lethal, based on his experience of earlier X-planes and the loss of Capt Milburn Apt in the X-2's capsule in 1956, and he argued for a conventional, lightweight rocket seat. He felt that the "X-15 was probably its own best capsule," and the pilot would be safer staying with the aircraft until it could be recovered to a suitable altitude and speed for normal ejection.

When the USAF inspected the X-15 mock-up it contained a very substantial, complex ejection seat with improved pilot restraint harness, stabilizing vanes to prevent tumbling after ejection and a 3,000lb-thrust rocket to push the seat clear of the aircraft. No objections were raised. The seat was extensively tested in 1958 but it took almost a year, until March 1959, to make it a reliable device that could offer a good chance of survival at Mach 4 and 120,000ft. No other seat came close to offering this possibility at that time.

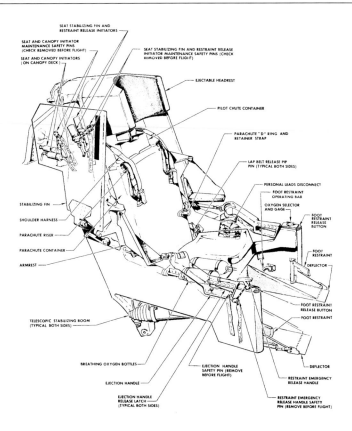

The X-15 ejection seat. At a USAF briefing Scott Crossfield explained that the shape of the 270lb seat (or "electric chair" as Milt Thompson saw it) derived from agricultural harvesters, offering light weight, correct posture, and relative comfort during the X-15's short but potentially turbulent flights. It was, he said, an example of "getting right down to fundamentals … typical of our thinking on this airplane." The seat was non-adjustable, requiring personally fitted foam pads for each pilot. It was designed to operate at altitudes below 125,000ft and speeds above Mach 3, although emergencies were likely to occur higher and faster than that. (North American Aviation)

LANDING

The choice of landing gear reflected X-2 experience in using a combination of manually retractable skids and a nose-wheel rather than the tricycle-wheeled undercarriage of the X-1 and D-558, or an all-skid arrangement as used by the Messerschmitt Me 163 and French SNCASE SE.5003 Baroudeur. The X-15's nose-gear consisted of twin magnesium wheels on a short, retracting shock strut with nitrogen-filled tires inflated to $240lb/in^2$, later increased to $295lb/in^2$. An air-scoop door popped open to pull down the main door aerodynamically, helping to deploy the nose-wheel unit. Two steel skids on Inconel-X struts folded forward against the aft rear fuselage. Initially they were to be located at the mid-fuselage position, but an aft position was eventually chosen, with the skids being released by a handle in the cockpit that opened up-locks and allowed bungees to extend the skids by gravity, like the nose-gear. There were no cockpit "green lights" to indicate extension, the pilot relying instead on visual confirmation from a chase pilot, knowing that ejection was the only alternative if the undercarriage failed to lower.

Full-scale tests showed that skids could be used to land on a conventional runway, although this was never necessary. On the sun-baked sediment of dry lakes where all the landings were made, it was calculated that the skids would last for about four landings. Shimmy dampers and torque links initially fitted to the nose-gear were found to be unnecessary, but the unit's shock strut compression and extension would cause problems later.

SUITED FOR SPACE

Exploration of very high altitudes required full-pressure suits to protect pilots in conditions in which severely reduced air pressure would cause the liquids in a human body to burst out through the skin. Pressure suits were originated by Dr. James Henry of the University of Southern California, working with a small company run by the highly innovative, quick-thinking, chain-smoking David Clark. Clark's main activity was the design and manufacturing of ladies' supportive under-garments, but during World War II he ventured into protective clothing and anti-g suits for aircrew. He manufactured a partial-pressure suit to Henry's specifications for use by early X-1 pilots Jack Woolams, Chuck Yeager

X-15-1 with a reduced AoA just before landing. Plenty of "forward stick" was needed after the skids touched down to bring the nose down too, and it would drop abruptly at around 6g. The aircraft's rear end could then lift off briefly, straining the undercarriage. When the aircraft halted a helicopter passed overhead to check for propellant leaks or smoke, and then dropped off a technician to open the canopy and "safe" the ejection seat. A convoy of support vehicles, led by a fire crew, arrived moments later. (AFFTC)

Inside the X-15

Most of the X-15's structure consisted of fuel tanks, virtually solid flying surfaces and a compact engine compartment in the tail. The nose area principally contained the cockpit, ball nose unit, instrument bay, nose-gear and stable platform.

Key

1 Q-ball sphere
2 Q-ball mounting collar
3 Q compensators, transducers and hydraulic valves.
4 Airspeed and altitude recorder
5 Undercarriage scoop door
6 Nose gear door
7 Ram air door
8 Ejection seat foot restraints
9 Telescopic seat stabilizing booms
10 Ejection handle
11 Liquid nitrogen cooling system
12 MH-96 adaptive controllers and accelerometers
13 Radar beacon antenna
14 Lower equipment compartment
15 UHF antenna
16 Control runs (inside fairing)
17 APU compartment
18 Stable platform location
19 APU exhausts (left and right)
20 Breathing oxygen disconnect point
21 Nitrogen disconnect point
22 Stellar cameras (oblique and vertical)

23 Forward experiment bay
24 Forward connecting link to NB-52 pylon
25 16mm internal cockpit camera
26 Seat stabilizing fin
27 Ballistic rocket seat catapult
28 Ejectable headrest
29 Parachute container
30 Central control column

31 Main instrument panel
32 Pitot
33 Nose gear strut (shortened on retraction)
34 Dual-ply Type VI EHD nose-wheel tyres
35 Insulating lining
36 Ballistic control system pitch and yaw vents

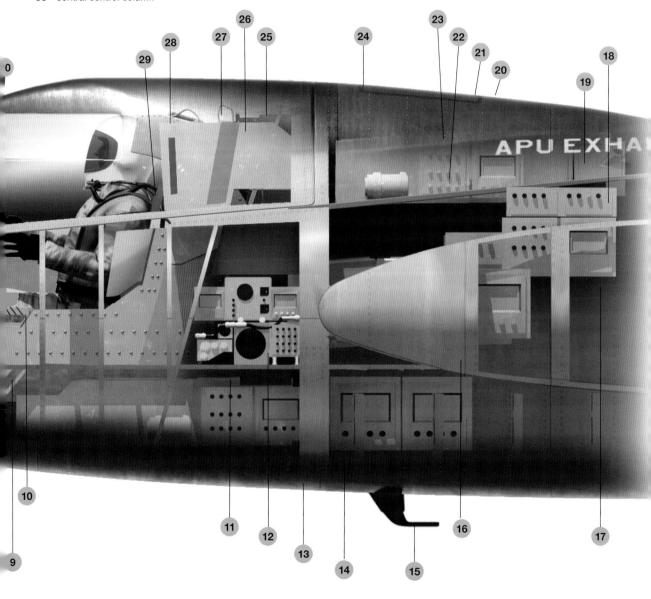

and Pete Everest, and the latter's life was saved by the suit when his X-1 cockpit de-pressurized at 65,000ft. This, the first emergency use of a partial-pressure suit, impressed the USAF, and it duly became the air force's standard T-1 suit, used (with considerable discomfort) by many high-altitude crews.

Clark's first full-pressure suit was for a US Navy contract in the early 1950s, and it was initially used in August 1953 by test pilot Lt Col Marion Carl, who climbed above 83,000ft in the D-558-II. The US Navy, however, subsequently chose a B. F. Goodrich design. The USAF realized that it too needed a full-pressure suit for use above 55,000 ft and Clark won the contract with a suit that weighed only 35lb. The first examples of the XMC-2 suit, including kangaroo-leather boots, were delivered for evaluation in December 1957 after a prolonged campaign by Crossfield, who insisted on the Clark suit rather than the USAF's preferred partial-pressure model. Its final configuration was not decided until May 1958, and six production examples were ordered from January 1959, each one individually "tailored."

The definitive MC-2, using Clark's patented "Link-net" material to facilitate movement, consisted of an inner ventilation suit with a wool insulation layer and upper and lower rubber garments folded together as a seal at the waist. The lower section also acted as an anti-g suit, effective up to 7g, while the upper part had built-in gloves. Both the cockpit and the suit were pressurized with nitrogen to reduce fire risk. The suit's rubber neck seal prevented nitrogen leaking into the pilot's fiberglass MA-3 helmet, which was supplied with 100 percent oxygen, as were the internal inflatable bladders that restrained the pilot's body during rapid acceleration. In the X-15 high-g acceleration, pressing on the pilot's body from chest to back, was experienced even in straight and level flight. When the engine lit up the force was 2g, but it increased to an uncomfortable 4g as the fuel burned off and the lightened aircraft continued to surge forward with almost 60,000lb of thrust.

Oxygen came from the NB-52's reserves during the ascent to launching altitude, but it was then switched to a bottled supply beneath the X-15's ejection seat. Expired air passed into the nitrogen-filled suit areas through a one-way valve in the neck seal, but problems occurred in balancing the pressure differences between the oxygen in the helmet and the nitrogen in the rest of the suit. The MC-2's aluminized, reflective outer layer gave it the "silver space-suit" appearance that was to become so familiar during the US manned space program. It housed the pilot's harness and parachute links and added some further insulation. The suit's relatively fragile texture was expected to absorb any damage during ejection.

David Clark continued to develop the suit, and by July 1960 offered a new and more comfortable A/P22S-2 model, with a new pressure-sealing zip fastener, in which all the layers (apart from the outer aluminized layer) formed one garment. This greatly simplified maintenance and "suiting up" for the pilot. A new helmet (referred to as "the hat"), with improved oxygen pressurization, incorporated a face seal in place of the neck seal, allowing better vision and easier neck movement. Its Sierracin visor had an electrical de-misting coating between two layers of stretched acrylic material. The pilot's gloves were separate from the suit, and his biomedical data was automatically recorded by sensors within the suit and passed to a data interface on the seat through a single electrical lead.

The A/P22S-2 was used for X-15 flights from March 21, 1961, after 36 flights using the MC-2, and it became the standard high-altitude suit for NASA and the US forces. In either suit the pilot could not remove his gloves or faceplate in flight. He could hear very little, and reaching some of the cockpit switches and the throttle became difficult – a problem when a delay of half a second in operating the controls could upset the flight plan. He also required groundcrew assistance to undo the many harness fittings post-flight.

SUPERSONIC SIMULATION

The final, crucial component in the program was the X-15 simulator that enabled pilots to plan and predict the flight characteristics of each mission with unprecedented care and accuracy. One of the program's principal innovations was the extensive use of simulation in the engineering of the aircraft itself and in the planning and analysis of its flights. It enabled designers to predict factors such as heating loads, flight emergency situations or the use of flying controls at the edge of the atmosphere.

By the end of 1956 NAA had constructed a strange-looking "Iron Bird" that included an X-15 cockpit on a skeletal frame with simplified X-15 electrical and hydraulic systems. Powered by analogue computers and capable of yaw, pitch and roll movement, this simulator could eventually reproduce flight characteristics at speeds up to Mach 8 using digital computers rescued from the Dyna-Soar program.

The US Navy made a particularly useful contribution to this phase of the X-15 program via its Aviation Medical Acceleration Laboratory at the Naval Air Development Center (NADC) in Johnsville, Pennsylvania. The latter's very advanced human centrifuge, opened in 1952, could generate forces of up to 40g (NADC "guinea pig" R. Flanagan Marshall withstood 31.25g for five seconds) and it enabled X-15 pilots to sit in a basic cockpit gondola assembly and experience the acceleration they would face in practice.

Johnsville technicians adapted their machine to simulate, for example, an emergency X-15 re-entry to the atmosphere with failed pitch dampers where the pilot was subjected to rapid changes of acceleration between 4 and 8g. Operating the controls under such forces became extremely difficult, and in one test Scott Crossfield, the first X-15 pilot to use the centrifuge, blacked out completely. One outcome was the rearrangement of some of the X-15's cockpit instruments to make them more visible and accessible under high-g conditions. X-15 pilots faced many visits to this torture chamber, with 1,000 simulations in May to July 1958 alone.

For actual flight training, the most useful simulator was the F-104 Starfighter, which also served as the main chase aircraft for the X-15 flights. Its small wing had similar wing loading to an X-15 in the landing phase, and pilots spent many hours in F-104s practicing landings. Several NASA F-104Ns and other Air Force Flight Test Center (AFFTC) Starfighters were used. A YF-100A was also involved, with its drag 'chute extended in flight before landing, and a Lockheed NT-33A (50-01420) was borrowed from the Cornell Aeronautical Laboratory.

With no experience of re-entering the atmosphere, it was not known how severely unstable the X-15 might become, or whether a pilot would be able to maintain control. The NT-33A was equipped with a variable stability system in an extended nose and a front cockpit that was a simplified X-15 type with side-stick controllers. The sensitivity of the flying controls could be varied in pitch, yaw and roll, and it would be flown in a zoom climb that would give about a minute at zero g, with the pilot's outside vision blanked off. The X-15's long fuselage and small wing area made it particularly sensitive in roll, but the ballistic control simulation showed only variations in pitch angle on the pilot's instrument panel and he had to try and maintain a stable flight attitude and correct speed even when SAS damper malfunctions and other control failures were simulated. Meanwhile, a second pilot in the rear seat maintained control of the NT-33A using conventional controls.

Joe Engle brings X-15-3 home after a September 28, 1960 flight to test three types of heat-proofing ablator coatings. The accompanying AFFTC F-104A (56-0768) was flown by fellow X-15 pilot "Pete" Knight, this aircraft being one of three F-104As and F-104Ns assigned to this flight. The X-15's glide ratio on approach was 4.5-to-1, so the accompanying F-104 had to be flown with throttle at idle, speed-brakes extended and flaps at the takeoff position for a sink rate of 18,000ft per minute at 345mph. The landing pattern began with arrival over the runway in the "high key" position at 23,000–30,000ft and at up to 345mph. After a 360-degree spiral turn, the aircraft was at about 20,000ft ("low key") and five miles abeam the runway. Remaining propellants were dumped and the tanks pressurized to prevent collapse as the pilot made a final 180-degree turn at 15,000ft. The lower ventral was jettisoned at 345mph and flaps and landing gear lowered for touchdown within about three minutes of reaching "high key." Smoke from the landing-strip markers is visible in the foreground. (AFFTC)

CHAPTER THREE

THREE BLACK BIRDS

X-15-1 powers away from the cameraman. XLR-11 motors were used until February 7, 1961 when Bob White took this aircraft to Mach 3.50, the fastest flight with these interim engines. Under power, the X-15 was considered relatively docile, although its behavior as a glider was harder to control – Bob White accused it of handling "like a water buffalo." On re-entry from high altitude, its stability reduced as the speed fell away, with quite severe tail buffeting at around 20 degrees AoA. Re-entry in a 40-degree dive at Mach 5.4 led to a pull-out in ten-degree increments, with the pilot sustaining 3g for around 20 seconds. When the MH-96 adaptive control system was installed it was a considerable help in maintaining control. (AFFTC)

By January 1958 the West High Bay section of NAA's Inglewood, California, factory had three sleek X-15s in various stages of assembly. Refining the NA-240 design had required more than 6,000 engineering drawings, cost $120 million and involved the modification of 200 sub-contracted items. Most of the manufacturing processes, particularly the challenging metalwork with new materials, were done by NAA. The unusual hardness of Inconel-X and titanium wore out tools quickly and required much longer times for polishing and cutting than conventional aviation metals. Nevertheless, by October 15, 1958 – two weeks ahead of schedule – the first aircraft, X-15-1 (56-6670), was ready for rollout, presided over by NAA vice-president Raymond Rice.

US vice-president Richard Nixon announced to the assembled guests, including six future X-15 pilots, that the new aircraft had "recaptured the US lead in space." He was also heard to comment through an inadvertently live microphone, "That sure is a funny looking thing." Harrison Storms declared that:

"The rollout of the X-15 marks the beginning of man's most advanced assault on space. In the X-15 we have all the elements and most of the problems of a true space vehicle. The performance of the X-15 is hard to comprehend. It can out-fly the fastest fighters by a factor of three, a high-speed rifle bullet by a factor of two and easily exceed the world altitude record by many times."

Those claims would take a while to realize as the aircraft still awaited their XLR-99 engines, and they used XLR-11s for the first phase of flight testing. Their combined thrust of 11,800lb from eight rocket chambers at sea level fell far short of the XLR-99's massive power, but

NAA X-15-1 66-670, Edwards AFB, California, April 19, 1960

Accompanied by fellow X-15 pilots Rushworth, McKay and Knight in F-100 and F-104 chase aircraft, Joe Walker used all eight XLR-11 chambers on April 19, 1960 during Flight 1-5-10 in this aircraft to reach Mach 2.56 and test stability, fuselage "tunnel" fairing vibration and flutter. Majs Fitzhugh Fulton and Jack Allavie flew launch NB-52A 52-003.

A fashion parade of David Clark A/P22S-2 suits, worn by six of the 12 X-15 pilots. They are, from left to right, Capt Joe Engle (USAF), Maj Bob Rushworth (USAF), Jack McKay (NASA), Maj "Pete" Knight (USAF), Milt Thompson (NASA) and Cdr Forrest Petersen (US Navy). Although the average age of the pilot team was under 40 (Neil Armstrong was 29), all had military experience, five had World War II combat time and three flew in the Korean War. All had college degrees and test pilot experience, in four cases on previous rocket-powered aircraft. They ran the risks of hypersonic flight on salaries that were usually half those of airline pilots. (AFFTC)

they were proven, reliable motors that would see further use in NASA's lifting body program. Installing them in the X-15 was relatively easy, although ethyl alcohol and water had to replace anhydrous ammonia in the fuel tanks.

HIGH, DRY RANGE

The location and facilities of Edwards AFB ('Eddy' to some pilots) were essential to X-15 operations. Situated 100 miles northeast of Los Angeles, the 44 square miles of Rogers Dry Lake (a pluvial lake or "playa") provided a smooth, hard landing surface for aircraft that could not operate from standard runways. Its clay and silt surface allowed longer, faster landing runs than normal runways and its remote location in the Mojave Desert gave classified projects relative secrecy. Dry for most of the year, its surface was washed and leveled by seasonal winter rain.

It had been used occasionally by the US Army Air Corps and US Army Air Force since 1933, but the great increase in flight testing during World War II brought 100 personnel to the hot, dusty base to introduce the USAAF's first jet fighter, the Bell XP-59A, in 1942 and the world's first supersonic flight by the XS-1 in October 1947. Joint NACA-USAF test programs began in 1946, and a rapid build-up of facilities and test programs continued into the Cold War years. The base, formally called Muroc, was renamed Edwards AFB in December 1949 to honor the loss of Capt Glen Edwards in 1948 when his Northrop YB-49 "Flying Wing" crashed.

In June 1951 the AFFTC was established at the base, with extensive new buildings and a 15,000ft concrete runway. Investment was needed for monitoring X-15 flights, which would require much more extensive airspace than previous rocket-plane tests, most of which had been conducted in the Edwards area. Hypersonic X-15 operations needed a long, clear aerial corridor, with radar, telemetry and communications sites at various points and a series of smaller dry lakes en route for emergency landing areas.

The USAF had allowed $1.5m (a serious underestimate) to establish a radar/telemetry range, and in May 1955 it was agreed that NACA would operate the sites and equipment involved. Telemetry would monitor basic aircraft and engine performance, but also the aircraft's structural and flight path characteristics and its airframe temperatures, as well as physiological data on the pilots and even research data on atmospheric features such as cosmic radiation. By November 1955 a 400-mile corridor had been selected from Wendover, Utah, to Edwards, avoiding heavily populated areas and airline routes and passing over barren terrain. Tracking stations were to be set up at Edwards, as well as in Ely and Beatty, Nevada, to constitute the High Altitude Continuous Tracking Range, or "High Range," under Project 1876 of March 1956.

Building the tracking sites raised its own problems. Ely, located at an altitude in excess of 8,000ft to give its World War II-vintage SCR-584 Mod II radar the clearest line of sight, required the building of a 5.6-mile road and installation of electricity generators. Water had to be trucked in, as it did for the Beatty site, which also needed its own electricity supply and an access road to its 4,900ft-high location. The Edwards end of the chain was installed in a 2,500sq ft extension to the third floor of Building 4800 at the base.

The radar sets had 10ft parabolic dishes, optical trackers and provision for 80in boresight cameras. Azimuth and elevation data for the test flights came from Baldwin analogue-to-digital optical encoders, and each site had a Model 205J plotting board to show the X-15's position according to plots from its site radar, although the radar data showing the course of each flight was usually recorded on large paper charts.

The selection of contingency landing sites, or "strange lakes" was necessary in case the X-15 pilot had to abort his flight soon after launch due to an emergency such as motor failure, although they were only used for ten of the 199 X-15 flights. The short gliding range of an X-15 at low altitude dictated the use of several smaller dry lakes that were fortuitously situated along the flight corridor. Launch points from the B-52 were chosen to give the pilot a down-wind landing pattern from a point roughly 19 miles from a lake bed, allowing enough distance to make a 180-degree reciprocal turn and land within the limited area of the lake. The X-15 simulator was used to calculate the relevant glide ranges, and ten possible launch points were identified using eight dry lakes – between 30 and 50 miles apart – as contingency landing sites, although the majority of flights ended at Edwards.

Tests on the potential dry lake sites began in 1957. Some were in the public domain and had to be fenced off to exclude livestock and provided with access roads. Others, such as Mud Lake or Groom Lake ("The Ranch"), both in Nevada, were in restricted areas used by the Atomic Energy Commission or for secret CIA "black projects." Although some lakes were covered in debris from use as bombing ranges, the crucial test was to establish whether the surface could support a landing. The testing device was an 18lb steel ball, dropped from a height of six feet at several points. The resulting depressions in the surface were measured and an impression of 3.25 inches or below was considered acceptable in assessing hardness. Future X-15 pilot Maj Bob White and AFFTC flight test chief Lt Col Clarence "Bud" Anderson flew a Helio L-28 Super Courier light aircraft, testing 12 lake surfaces and only once having to make an emergency go-around when the undercarriage wheels began to sink into silt.

For the first phase of testing, with XLR-11 motors, Silver Lake, Bicycle Lake, Cuddeback and Harper's Lake were cleared for use. For later, longer-ranging tests more distant lakes were needed, and Hidden Hills Ranch, Three Sisters and Smith Ranch were added, although several others were also assessed.

Each emergency lake required complex support arrangements,

Milton O. Thompson with a relatively smart-looking X-15-3. Emergency, servicing and other markings usually melted off and had to be repainted after virtually every flight. Turning the X-15 around for another flight usually took 10 to 14 days. Thompson joined NACA's High Speed Flight Station in March 1956 as one of only five NACA pilots – the latter included future X-15 flyers Joe Walker, Neil Armstrong and Jack McKay. Thompson flew the X-15 14 times. (AFFTC)

and these were specified by Paul Bikle, Director of the NASA Flight Research Center at Edwards, in October 1960. A team would be placed at the designated lake with two 500-gallon fire trucks, a Piasecki H-21 Shawnee helicopter and personnel including firemen, a doctor, USAF specialists on pressure suits and X-15 maintenance and a pilot to act as lake controller. They were required to move in the day before a mission. Similar, smaller teams would be emplaced at two other potential landing sites, and a C-130 Hercules would be waiting on the runway at one of them to evacuate the pilot for medical treatment if necessary. F-104 chase aircraft patrolled the landing site to guide the X-15 pilot in safely. Another specialist team waited at Edwards with similar equipment and more F-104s. NASA actually requested greater support for each launch, including three C-130s to transport the vehicles and four paramedics, but this exceeded AFFTC's resources.

The lake beds also had to have 300ft-wide runways marked out on them with 8ft-wide edge lines of tar, helping the X-15 pilot to judge his altitude on approach. Marked runways were two or three miles long, and markings had to be renewed each year after the winter rains. The hardness of the surface was frequently checked using a motorcycle, a NASA R4D (C-47) or a T-33. Judging firmness from the air was impossible, and one test landing went wrong when an aircraft flown by Chuck Yeager and Neil Armstrong sank axle-deep into mud. A test landing by Armstrong on another occasion tore the tip-tank, ventral fin and radio antenna off his F-104, the future astronaut having to rapidly engage the jet's afterburner to escape from the soft surface. Clearly each X-15 launch was going to be a complex and extremely expensive adventure, placing even greater pressure on the team to minimize technical failures.

CHASING SPACEMEN

Like previous rocket-plane programs, the X-15 required chase aircraft to observe the launch and recovery stages of each flight. A total of 741 chase flights were eventually made, 533 of them by F-104s. Although the X-15 quickly left its observers behind once it had gathered speed and altitude, the "chasers" were invaluable in checking for exterior problems early in the flight and for guiding the black "glider" in to a safe landing.

Typically, between three and five chase aircraft were needed per flight. Chase One, originally one of four F-100s, but from 1961 a Northrop T-38A (or, occasionally, ex-US Navy Douglas F5D Skylancers, two of which had been acquired by NASA), took off with the carrier aircraft and stayed with it on the flight to the launch point. Its pilot, often another X-15-trained aviator, worked through the pre-launch checklists with the X-15 pilot, watching for control surface movements, jettisoning of propellants and engine-priming procedures.

Chase Two usually flew a NASA F-104, which cruised better at lower altitudes. It was positioned near a potential launch lake to assist in an emergency landing. Chase Three, another F-104, supported Chase Two, but took off later to conserve fuel and orbited near launch lake sites. Its pilot would accompany the X-15 on landing, calling out altitudes and checking for correct deployment of the landing gear and lower ventral fin jettisoning. The F-104 was the only available type that could follow the X-15 closely on landing. Over Edwards, Chase Four would be in position to provide the same approach and landing assistance at close quarters, having accelerated in afterburner to intercept the X-15 after detecting the white vapor trail as its excess propellants were jettisoned. Each flight was filmed from a two-seat Chase One F-100F or T-38A or a fifth jet, which could dash ahead of the X-15 just before launch.

FIRST FLIGHTS

Before the X-15 first became airborne on March 10, 1959, there was lengthy discussion between NACA and AFFTC about the division of responsibilities. Walt Williams at NACA nurtured some mistrust of the USAF's participation, rooted in NACA's judgment that the air force had rushed the last stages of the X-2 program for publicity purposes, with fatal consequences. A meeting with Capt Iven Kincheloe, the USAF's first designated X-15 pilot, on May 24, 1957, established that AFFTC wanted as much of the flying as possible, but its lack of technical qualification on the X-15 dictated cooperation with NACA. Williams, aware that the USAF was paying most of the bill, still maintained that NACA had primary responsibility for the program in view of its role in researching the X-15's structural and flight characteristics.

By 1959 an X-15 Joint Operations Committee had been set up and it specified the division of tasks. NASA would maintain the three X-15s and provide data collection, the High Range monitoring chain, and some chase aircraft. AFFTC took responsibility for the NB-52s, the pilots' survival gear, the rocket motors, support aircraft, landing areas, and some of the tracking radars. Other roles were shared.

Thoroughness in background preparation and flight simulation enabled flying to begin with greatly reduced risks from stability and control problems, which had occurred during the earlier X-plane programs. With two X-15s at Edwards by early 1959, extensive ground testing continued, with particular emphasis on curing troublesome components such as the two auxiliary power units (APUs). They operated by pouring hydrogen peroxide over a bed of silver crystal oxidizer, reducing the peroxide to steam and oxygen for the turbines to generate electrical and hydraulic power.

Although X-15-1 was mated to its NB-52A pylon in the first week of January 1959, company test pilot Scott Crossfield had to wait until March 10 for his first flight while additional ground testing was conducted. Finally, at 1000hrs on the 10th, Charlie Bock and Jack Allavie eased the NB-52A into the hot Mojave air at 198mph and 258,000lb for a captive flight lasting just over an hour. The combination flew well, as the wind-tunnel tests had predicted. Crossfield, in a full-pressure suit, checked the flying controls and airspeed data from the flight test boom. At 35,000ft he tested the suit and the flight continued up to 45,000ft and Mach 0.85. He found that he could still reach and operate all the controls, including the ram-air door which de-pressurized the cockpit.

Increased landing weights prompted the installation of a third skid for the first and third X-15s in 1966–67. Operated by hydraulic cylinders, it extended below the ventral stabilizer. Frictional heat was absorbed by the desert floor rather than the skids. Smoke pots were ignited along the edge of the runway to make it more visible on approach and show wind direction. A second set had to be lit 30 seconds before the aircraft landed – a challenging task for the smoke-pot lighters who could see the black "predator" approaching at 200mph. (NASA Dryden)

The next three flights were also captive-carry examples as technical problems prevented the glide test intended for the second flight. On two of them frustrating APU faults recurred, with leaks and pressurization difficulties that would continue to some extent throughout the program. The APUs were repeatedly modified and partially redesigned, but they and the regulators and valves, particularly in the hydrogen peroxide system, were hard to perfect. Crossfield sat in the X-15-2 cockpit for ground runs of the XLR-11 installation on May 22, 1959 and attempted a glide flight once more on June 5, but thick smoke in the cockpit caused another abort.

Another fault occurred three days later when the yellow SAS pitch damper malfunction light came on as the X-15-1 finally separated from the NB-52A's pylon at 0838hrs, but Crossfield proceeded with the flight. He knew that further delays would erode the reputation of a program that was much more public than the preceding, semi-secret X-plane operation. After the shock of Sputnik, as he put it "The X-15 has become an important symbol of our national scientific ability – or lack of it. A simple mistake could severely tarnish the national image." Besides, press reporters were watching the day's activities closely. The APUs were working well and everything else was "up" as Crossfield grasped the side controller, engaged one degree of nose-up trim and counted down to the moment when the three shackles holding the X-15 released it with a metallic "clunk." He decided to use his five minutes of flying time to get the "feel" of the X-15 and then made a wide "S" turn and spiraled down.

The Rocket Engine Test Facility at Edwards AFB, with the first X-15 in a similar situation to X-15-3 when it exploded on June 8, 1960. Although the design was not at fault, the incident was a dramatic reminder of the precarious nature of its propellants. A full load of liquid oxygen had a drastic effect on other materials around it. For example, it reduced the temperature of the hydraulic oil in the control system to minus 80 degrees F – close to a temperature that would have rendered the controls inoperative. Before one flight an access door, removed for repair, was left in the sun and expanded to its normal size. To make it fit back into place on the aircraft's frozen skin it had to be soaked in a bucket of liquid nitrogen to shrink it. Any gaps in the panels had to be covered by metal strips to stop superheated air from entering, burning wires and aluminum tubing. (AFFTC)

His first attempt to establish level flight with the side controller resulted in a severe porpoising oscillation, but gentle control movements steadied it up at 36,000ft and 300mph. Orange-tailed F-100 chase planes followed him down as he rapidly lost altitude, and Bob White confirmed that the X-15's lower ventral fin had parachuted away at 6,000ft. On approach at 600ft, Crossfield noticed the unexpected difficulty of visual distortion caused by looking through two layers of windshield and the glass of the helmet visor. It affected his depth perception as he peered out at the black runway lines.

At 200mph the porpoising motion began again and proved impossible to correct as the X-15 sank rapidly towards the desert. Crossfield lowered the landing gear and flaps, but he was concerned that he might "break the bird" as its instability continued, so he overshot his intended landing point by half a mile and tried to flare the landing at a low point in one of the oscillations. The skids finally made contact, bending two bell-cranks in their mechanism and the nose immediately slammed down as the X-15 skidded for another mile, leaving a plume of dust.

The familiar post-landing scenario then commenced, with a cavalcade of ambulances, fire trucks, Air Police and other cars, the yellow David Clark suiting-up vehicle and the Mobile Control van all heading off in a dust storm to surround the now-inert blue-black stiletto. The H-21 helicopter ferried in Dr. Toby Freedman to do the first checks on Crossfield, whose main concern was to establish with Harrison Storms why the X-15, so stable in theoretical tests and simulations, had almost lost control on landing. "Stormy," first on the scene, assured Crossfield that the oscillations did not indicate basic design problems.

It was soon found that, in addition to the pitch damper problem, slow control response was the real cause, attributable to inadequate pressure in the hydraulic system powering the flying controls. Additional power was routed through valves from other systems and the difficulty did not recur. Remedial work was done immediately as X-15-1 was already due for minor improvements and preparation for powered flight. At 296.6 seconds, the June 8 flight was the shortest of the program, and one of the slowest and lowest at 522mph and 37,550ft.

The focus then moved to X-15-2 (56-6671) and ground tests of its XLR-11 motors at the Rocket Engine Test Facility, where the aircraft was anchored to a concrete base and filled with nine tons of lox and "walc" (water/alcohol mixture, or as Crossfield saw it "6,000 fifths of pure vodka"). Here, the crew ran a practice launch and rocket start procedure. Early attempts were interrupted by repeated problems with the complex oxygen tank regulator valve. After one test technicians began to purge the hydrogen peroxide lines with nitrogen. Sadly, the new nitrogen hose had a thin film of oil that reacted violently with the peroxide and started a blaze that burned out the aircraft's engine bay and badly injured a crewman.

After several weeks of repairs, X-15-2 was ready for a captive-carry flight in which it would carry and jettison a full load of propellants

for the first time. This costly process had to be demonstrated, as the aircraft's weight and stress limits meant that it could only land safely without propellants aboard. Although the oxygen top-off process was incomplete, all the propellants were vented inside the time limits of 140 seconds for the peroxide and 110 seconds for the rest. However, continuing APU, regulator valve and hydraulic faults caused further wasted flights and delays throughout August and September, resulting in immense frustration for the X-15 team.

Under pressure from his bosses at NAA and the USAF at Wright Field, Storms defended the cautious approach and its aim of avoiding

ABOVE
Scott Crossfield brings the overweight X-15-2 into Rosamund Dry Lake emergency landing site on November 5, 1959 after a rocket chamber explosion. Seconds later the nose of the overweight aircraft slammed down hard, fracturing the fuselage at Station 226.8. To one journalist the aircraft took on the appearance of "a chicken squatting to alight" as it approached the lake bed. (AFFTC)

Groundcrew make the damaged X-15-2 safe after its landing accident in which about three-quarters of the bolts securing the fuselage at the break-point were sheared off. (NASA)

"the loss of either millions of dollars of equipment or a pilot." NAA had missed its deadline of delivering a fully capable X-15 to NASA within four years and repeated attempts at powered flight had been aborted. It was also concerned that it had just lost the deal for the F-108 interceptor in September 1959. NAA's other vital contract, the XB-70 Valkyrie bomber, would be canceled by March 1961 after the expenditure of $800m mainly because of the absorption of funds by the hugely expensive ICBM program.

On September 17 fortune smiled at last and Crossfield, in X-15-2, took on a final lox top-up from Bill Berkowitz in the NB-52A at 0756hrs and started the APUs. Apart from low pressure in the nitrogen cooling for the electronics bay and a brief, last-minute, over-pressure in the lox tank, everything was running well and Crossfield flashed the green "launch" light on Bock's B-52 instrument panel. Within 2,000ft from the drop all eight XLR-11 chambers were lit and at 33,000ft the aircraft started to climb, with Bock giving steering instructions as the X-15 had no compass. The chase F-104s were soon left far behind and Crossfield was relieved to find that the black aircraft flew well with either the center stick or side controller in use.

Leveling out at 50,000ft, he performed several turns and rolls, including a full aileron roll. Within three minutes from launch Crossfield reached Mach 2.3, whereupon he shut down three chambers as contractor flights were not supposed to exceed Mach 2. With his fuel exhausted after four minutes, he headed for the lake, landing in a strong crosswind but with no pitch instability. Pushed off-course from the marked runway, the X-15 stopped just short of a drainage ditch that could have removed the undercarriage. As Crossfield began to exit the cockpit a fire broke out just above the ventral fin, where a cracked pump casing had leaked alcohol into the engine compartment. It was quickly extinguished but repairs took three weeks, and Crossfield was lucky that the fire had not erupted earlier in the flight.

Gremlins reappeared on the next two flights when launches were prevented by cockpit or lox tank pressurization problems, caused in one case by a frozen valve. Crossfield, however, got a good Mach 2.4 flight on October 17, during which he had a chance to explore roll and sideslip characteristics. Another potentially successful launch five days later was abandoned when Crossfield ripped one of his pressure suit gloves while trying to free a small, jammed oxygen valve. Moments later his windshield froze over with thick ice.

Bad weather delayed the next launch until November 5, when he was dropped at 44,000ft on what he had hoped would be the first trip from a distant launch point, 70 miles from Edwards. He lit six barrels of the XLR-11, but triggering the last two caused a violent jarring followed by a fire warning light. Crossfield shut down the other chambers and heard from close-in chase pilot Bob White (who had felt the explosion shake his F-104) that there was evidence of damage. Based on the experience of previous X-1 and X-2 rocket-planes, where

similar XLR-11 explosions had occurred, Crossfield should have ejected before the whole aircraft came apart. Instead, he began to jettison his fuel and headed for the diversionary Rosamund Dry Lake with flames streaming from the aircraft's tail. Because about 1,000lb remained in the tanks he knew he would have to make a heavy landing. However, the fire (caused by an engine ignition failure) appeared to be out and he was able to make a normal touchdown at 185mph, but the nose banged down much harder than usual and the landing run was only 1,500ft rather than 5,000ft.

The medics aboard the rescue helicopter had heard mention of a "broken back" and misunderstood, assuming that Crossfield, rather than the X-15, had "broken" and they duly rushed forward with a back-board ready to lift him out of the cockpit. Crossfield, unable to communicate as his helmet faceplate was still sealed, tried to hold down the heavy canopy to prevent it from arming and jettisoning while the rescuers did their best to pull it out of the way. Eventually, NAA flight surgeon Toby Freedman realized that the pilot's energetic efforts indicated an absence of serious injury, and he told Crossfield that his X-15 was "busted in two." The front 19ft of its fuselage had buckled upwards and the short landing run was caused by the rear section scooping down into the desert and dragging the rocket-plane to an abrupt halt.

It was established that the extra landing weight, together with the lack of shock absorption by the nose-gear, had caused the break. Extra doubling plates and fasteners were fitted to all X-15s in that area. Also, a slightly slower nose-gear extension sequence prevented oil in its shock absorber from foaming and losing its shock-absorbing properties, making for less brutal landings.

While X-15-2 returned to the Inglewood repair facility again, the first aircraft was ready to resume testing, still with XLR-11s and a nose-boom. After an aborted flight on December 16 when fuel tank pressure was lost, Crossfield made its first powered flight on January 23, 1960, reaching Mach 2.53 and 66,844ft. The aircraft was then handed over to NASA. This promising start to a new year contrasted with 1959 when nine of the 13 attempts at powered flight had been

X-15-2's XLR-99 lights up after launch. A routine soon developed in which the NB-52 turned onto its launch heading, facing Edwards AFB, at eight minutes before launch. Six minutes later, the X-15 pilot switched on data recording equipment, checked his "Q-ball" and ensured that the NB-52's launch cameras were on. After a countdown from ten the "drop" took place. If the motor would not light the X-15 could glide for up to 400 miles from high altitude. The captive flight stage was the most risky, as there was insufficient time to jettison propellants below 26,000ft. Had a problem arisen, the X-15 pilot would have had to eject while his aircraft was still on the pylon. (AFFTC) abandoned through technical failures and only one of the 15 NB-52 trips (including captive and glide flights) had resulted in a successful rocket-powered flight. Many faults had been cured, however, without terminal loss or damage, and vital experience had been gained to enable a high success rate in 1960, when 13 powered flights were completed (including the fastest flight ever made by a manned aircraft) in the first five months alone, with only three aborts.

GOLDEN YEAR FOR BLACK BIRDS

1960 began with the brief, annual rainfall that flooded the Edwards lake area and almost caused a move to Tonopah Dry Lake, in Nevada. After X-15-1's successful January 23 flight, Crossfield resumed testing with the second aircraft. Although its first outing on February 4 was only a captive flight due to familiar problems with the APU and tank pressure, it was airborne again on February 11. Flying the "long ride" from a Utah launch point, the rocket-plane zoomed to 90,000ft and leveled out at Mach 2.5. Crossfield performed a steep simulated re-entry dive, descending almost seven miles in 20 seconds. He tested the speed brakes at Mach 0.9, comparing their effect to "hitting a brick wall" and almost forgot to arm the jettisoning charge in the lower ventral, narrowly avoiding it ploughing into the lake bed on landing. On final approach Crossfield's oxygen regulator failed, and this would soon have prevented him from breathing within the cockpit's nitrogen atmosphere. Luckily, he was able to open the ram-air door and his helmet visor as soon as the aircraft stopped.

The last few XLR-11 flights were also generally successful, despite occasional engine shut-downs and an alcohol leak that ended the March 18 flight before launch. Crossfield felt sufficient confidence in X-15-2 to subject it to some fairly extreme maneuvers 11 days later, including a 6g pull-up and others at high angles of attack.

In preparation for the higher-altitude flights, a series of ground tests on the ballistic control system preceded a flight test on May 5 in which Crossfield found that, at lower altitude, the peroxide-generated steam from the nose ballistic ports covered the windshield rather than evaporating, icing it up. An APU failure confirmed an aborted launch.

Another new system was tested on Crossfield's 25th X-15 flight on May 26. He was wired up to the "physiological package" that was to be used by Project Mercury astronauts (NASA's main interest in 1960), measuring temperature, heart rate and breathing. It included a "rectal probe," which Crossfield understandably chose to omit. He resisted the temptation to increase his heart rate drastically by rapidly flexing his muscles and then pulling the plug on the system as a way of alarming the aero-medical officers on the ground. It proved to be a very successful flight, although his Mach 2.7 speed was well in excess of the set limits. Crossfield also re-tested the ballistic controls but found that they had no effect in the denser atmosphere at 50,000ft. The contractor test rules included a 100,000ft altitude limit, beyond which the ballistic jets would work.

It was also the last flight by an XLR-11-powered X-15. After 31 flights within five years of the submission of the first draft proposals for the aircraft – a much shorter development time than that of the X-2, X-3 or most of the Century Series fighters – X-15-2 was removed from the flightline for installation of its XLR-99 in June 1960.

THE BIG MOTOR

The first ground-test XLR-99 was delivered to Edwards' "Rocket Shop" on June 7, 1959 and testing began on August 26, with sound levels of 140 decibels for groundcrew to tolerate. Before that, on June 29, the third X-15 – the first to be equipped with the new engine from "birth" – was taken to Edwards and secured with steel clamps to a concrete test platform. Observers could watch engine runs from the safety of underground bunkers and monitor the performance through elaborate telemetry.

However, a pilot was required in the cockpit, and Crossfield reported for the third test, wearing his office clothes rather than an MC-2 suit, on June 8, 1960. He used a simple oxygen pack so that he could close the canopy and pressurize the cockpit to simulate a launch and motor light-up ahead of a flight, anticipated a month later. With everything working well, he started the engine at half-power and advanced the throttle to maximum thrust. The aircraft vibrated in the welter of noise for a short time before he shut it down as part of his "flight plan," although a valve malfunction light was showing.

The next step was a re-start, and he pressed the engine circuit reset switch to initiate a start. The aircraft instantly exploded as all 16,000lb of propellants detonated in a 30ft-diameter fireball, destroying the rear section and shooting the cockpit and nose 20ft across the test bay with forces approaching 20g. With great presence of mind, the

The rear skids of X-15-2 make contact at the end of the first flight with the XLR-99 motor, when Crossfield flew it to Mach 2.97 at 50 percent thrust on November 15, 1960 – his fastest speed in an X-15. Directional stability of the landing gear during landing run-outs was found to be much better than that of the X-2, although steering was very limited during the landing run, using the horizontal stabilizer and rudder. This was useful when Joe Engle had to maneuver X-15-3 past an F-4C Phantom II that was stuck on the Edwards runway in June 1965. However, there could be no brakes to control speed. A transport dolly lifted the rear fuselage to move the X-15 around on the ground. (AFFTC) uninjured Crossfield turned off the power supplies and braced himself for a second explosion. The fire truck arrived 30 seconds later to quell the blaze and Crossfield was somewhat reluctantly assisted from the relative safety of the cockpit. No-one else was injured, but much of the aircraft was lost, although the wings and nose section were repairable.

The explosion was caused by over-pressurization of the ammonia tank when a vapor-dispersal pipe venting the ammonia became blocked by a frozen valve and the tank ruptured, mixing its contents explosively with those of the damaged peroxide tank. Re-design of a valve and regulator were the only changes needed, and it was decided that a $4.75m rebuild of the aircraft was justified despite having to create most of the parts from scratch. The revised system was also built into X-15-2, which was having its XLR-99 installed at Inglewood. It was an opportunity to install a newly developed Minneapolis-Honeywell MH-96 adaptive control system into X-15-3, as well as the Nortronics "ball nose" sensors that had always been intended for the high-speed flight phase. The "ball," which did not measure speed, was combined with an airspeed probe just ahead of the cockpit.

MH-96 required a new instrument panel that was easier to use while wearing a pressure suit. It had Lear-Siegler vertical-tape displays, similar to those in the F-105 Thunderchief. Tested in a McDonnell F-101A Voodoo for the Dyna-Soar project, the system used gyros and electronic modules with an inertial platform to provide constant, automatic control damping in the pitch, roll and yaw axes whatever the conditions in which the controls were operated. It replaced the original Westinghouse SAS, controlling both aerodynamic and ballistic control systems and including autopilot functions. The pilot could still use the left side controller for manual ballistic control, but MH-96 could blend both types of control depending on the flight conditions. Although it was an experimental system it usually proved to be reliable in the X-15.

Scott Crossfield made the third and final XLR-99 test flight on December 6, 1960, demonstrating re-starts and effective throttling as well as high-g maneuvers at speeds up to Mach 2.85. When he lit up the engine the sound was audible to the B-52 crew above the roar of their eight engines. It was also the last flight with the nose instrument boom. Crossfield had successfully completed his manufacturer's flight program within a record total of 101 rocket-plane flights. He was subsequently transferred to NAA's Hound Dog missile program and then the Apollo space project. Crossfield's back-up pilot throughout the company test phase, Alvin S. White, who remained in constant preparation with simulator and chase pilot time, was never called upon to fly the X-15.

CHAPTER FOUR

THE ENVELOPE EXPANDS

The conclusion of the manufacturer's initial flight tests and the transfer of X-15-1 to NASA on February 3, 1960 began Phase II in which NASA and the USAF agreed to share the flight program, taking the aircraft to higher speeds and altitudes. Maj Robert M. White was given the high-speed flights while Joseph A. Walker from NASA was allocated the high-altitude program, although they actually flew both missions. Both pilots had long experience of fighters and Walker had flown several X-planes. Of the two operational X-15s, the first would be used to expand the performance envelope to the design limits while X-15-2 provided pilot training and undertook other research work.

Joe Walker made the first "government" flight on March 25, 1960, using X-15-1 with its XLR-11s. Bob White, who had worked with X-15 construction engineers to familiarize himself with the aircraft, followed up for the USAF on Friday, April 13, reaching Mach 1.9 and 48,000ft. The two pilots alternated flights for six months. During 1960 seven pilots made 27 full flights, White actually making 32 in all, although half were aborted.

The first launch from a remote lake took place on May 12 when Walker was dropped near Silver Lake in X-15-1, ascended to 77,882ft and made the first Mach 3 X-15 flight. At Mach 3.19 he switched off three chambers, but the abrupt deceleration caused the others to shut down as the fuel pumps cavitated. White flew even faster to Mach 3.5 on February 7, 1961 – the highest speed for an XLR-11-powered X-15 – and he achieved a new altitude record for piloted aircraft on August 12, 1960 when he soared to 136,500ft. He was launched from the

X-15-1 is prepared for transport back to the hangar after Neil Armstrong's familiarization flight on November 30, 1960. For the pilots, preparation for each flight involved two weeks of physical working-out and an alcohol-free diet. They often faced a gap of at least two months between flights. Unusually, Joe Walker made two flights in 11 days in April 1962, one of which set a new height record that reached twice the altitude of the previous record holder, a rocket-boosted MiG-21. The influx of new pilots meant that he had made only two X-15 flights in the previous 11 months. (AFFTC)

Bob White was denied his February 21, 1961 launch when the X-15-2's inertial platform failed, leaving it suspended below NB-52B 52-008. A large white patch of frost covers the lower fuselage below the lox tanks and there is an experimental infra-red coating on the dorsal rudder. (AFFTC)

NB-52 at 45,000ft and Mach 0.85 100 miles from Edwards. After ascending to 60,000ft with eight degrees AoA, he leveled off, accelerated to Mach 1.9 and pulled up into a steeper 15-degree climb. When the propellants ran out at 116,500ft the aircraft climbed ballistically to 136,500ft and White commented, "It's kinda empty up here." He then began re-entry, leveling out at 46,000ft to return home.

The US Navy's minor role in the project (the X-15 was not seen to have direct naval applications) was represented by Cdr Forrest S. Petersen, who joined the program enthusiastically as the fourth X-15 pilot from August 1958 until January 1962. He made five X-15 flights, three with the XLR-99 engine, and undertook the only chase flight made by an F4H-1 Phantom II. During Petersen's first flight the upper XLR-11 shut down soon after launch and he concluded from the rapid deceleration that the lower engine had also failed. He was guided back to Edwards by fellow X-15 pilot Milt Thompson at NASA-1 control and Joe Walker in an F-104. He arrived at the so-called "high key" position, where he would begin his landing approach, at only 25,000ft, and had to make a tight turn to enter final approach before performing a textbook landing.

Roger Barniki of NASA (who helped to design David Clark suits and "suited up" most X-15 pilots) arranged for US Navy insignia to be painted on the X-15-2 for Cdr Petersen's September 28, 1961 "heat" flight. Petersen was piped aboard the aircraft along a red carpet for a mission with airframe skin temperatures that exceeded 1,000 degrees F for the first time. (NASA)

Three new pilots joined White and Walker in Phase III tests from October 1960. World War II F6F Hellcat veteran Jack McKay joined NACA in 1951, testing Century Series fighters and flying the D-558, X-1B and X-1E. He had already made 46 rocket flights before joining the X-15 team – second only to Crossfield – and he was regarded as an excellent pilot. McKay made the first of 29 X-15 flights, including two with the XLR-11, in December. The USAF's Maj Bob Rushworth did his familiarization flight in November, followed by 34 more in the aircraft – the highest number

NAA X-15-2 66-671, Edwards AFB, California, November 9, 1961

During Flight 2-21-37 on November 9, 1961, Bob White exceeded Mach 6 for the first time on the X-15-2's 21st flight. Dropped from NB-52B 52-008 (flown by Maj Jack Allavie and Sqn Ldr Harry Archer of the RAF), the aircraft reached Mach 6.04 (4,093mph) and 101,600ft over Death Valley. As this profile shows, some areas of the fuselage, including the canopy, were coated with heat-resistant ablator.

for any X-15 pilot. A transport pilot in World War II, Rushworth had flown numerous high-performance jets with the Fighter Operations Branch at Edwards in the 1950s. The third newcomer was Neil Armstrong, a veteran of the Korean War, where he had flown US Navy F9F-2 Panthers in combat before returning to civilian life. He had subsequently spent many hours testing "hot" jets at NACA's High-Speed Flight Station before moving to the Dyna-Soar project. Armstrong made seven X-15 flights up to July 1962, when he was chosen for the second NASA astronaut class, leading to his selection as the first man on the Moon in July 1969's Apollo 11 mission.

MACH 4... 5... 6

As 1960 progressed the number of technical problems diminished, although APUs continued to throw up unexpected faults and oil leaks. A repeatedly frozen hydraulic reservoir was remedied by extra electric heaters. The first 1961 launch for X-15-2, which was also the first government flight with an XLR-99 under Test Phase IV, happened on March 7 when Bob White made the world's first Mach 4 flight (twice the speed of a rifle bullet), topping out at Mach 4.43 and 77,450ft. It was a useful exploration of stability and control at that speed, as well as structural heating: slight heat-induced buckling occurred to some side-tunnel panels, and this increased as speeds rose further still, requiring extra expansion joints in several panels. The "ball nose" worked well on its first flight test.

Joe Walker with the X-15-2. All flights were made on instruments as there were no visual references from the blue/black void visible during the climb to high altitude. The pilot could not see any external areas of his aircraft, just the window frames. High speed and acceleration could fool his senses, so rigid adherence to the instruments was vital or he might feel that the aircraft was over-rotating and about to flip over backwards. Back-up reference lines were marked inside the manually operated canopy to assist with this. (NASA)

Walker's first 1961 flight was interrupted by a telemetry failure to X-15-2. He landed, still attached to the NB-52's pylon, but the bomber's big braking parachute failed and its brakes severely overheated in a 12,000ft landing run, requiring a week of repairs.

A successful flight was possible on March 30, and Walker gave the new Clark A/P22S-2 suit its first use, reporting improved comfort and vision. He achieved an engine re-start moments after launch following a sudden shut-down (a common feature of most XLR-99 flights in 1961) and he scored another "first" by experiencing two minutes of weightlessness at the apex of his 169,000ft ascent. There was unforeseen, heavy vibration due to "structural resonance" as the SAS pitch gyro reacted to increased use of the flying controls to maintain stability on re-entry. For Walker, the more memorable aspects of the flight included the "very deep violet blue" of the atmosphere, as well as "an appreciation of different levels of the surface. Mountains still stand out as mountains" and the realization that the "curvature of the Earth was very apparent." Five weeks later Lt Cdr Alan Shepard made the first suborbital Project Mercury flight, and such observations soon became quite familiar for the public.

Heat-sensitive Detecto-Temp paint was applied to areas on the left side of the aircraft and on the right rudder surface for several flights. The discoloration showed the different heating levels absorbed by the airframe. (NASA)

Joe Walker made X-15-1's 24th free flight on October 17, 1961, reaching Mach 5.74 and an altitude of 108,600ft as he explored stability and control and aerodynamic heating. In the background, the faithful orange-striped AFFTC H-21C-PH Shawnee 51-15855 has landed to provide support personnel as Walker prepares to exit the cockpit and groundcrew change the nose-wheels to tow the X-15. (AFFTC)

During the 1961 flights most of the test objectives concerning aerodynamic heating and its effects on the X-15, hypersonic stability and the physiological reactions of the pilots were met. Wind-tunnel and theoretical work on heating could at last be backed up by actual flight experience. More exact data could also be obtained by the use of Detecto-Temp paint on selected areas of the airframe. Used earlier on the X-2, these multi-colored strips of heat-sensitive paint, together with thermocouples in other areas, revealed those parts of the aircraft's surface that were subject to extreme heating or acting as heat-sinks. Internal spars and ribs often stood out in the latter category. Minor structural changes, including extra fasteners and expansion slots, were made to the wings' leading edges where exceptionally high skin temperatures were recorded. Temperatures increased markedly with higher speeds – at Mach 6 the skin temperatures were eight times higher than those at Mach 3. Pilots recalled hearing the airframe emitting a range of percussive popping noises as it heated up beyond Mach 5.

In 1967 the Cold Wall experiment used an Inconel-X test panel attached to the right side of X-15-3's rudder which had an insulating cover that was jettisoned at high speed, subjecting the test panel to instantaneous hypersonic heating in order to measure the effects on its composition.

Re-entry profiles from high-altitude missions were tested in Phase V, and it was found that establishing a constant AoA at the top of the climb and gradually decreasing it as the aircraft approached level flight worked best. On the way up, as the altitude increased, so should the AoA to prevent over-stressing the airframe. Re-entry was possible without engaging SAS at an AoA approaching eight degrees but a back-up alternative SAS (ASAS) roll damper was installed, although the MH-96 in the third aircraft did not require one.

It was also concluded that the symmetrical arrangement of upper and lower vertical stabilizers was somewhat redundant. Originally, they were included to compensate for possible thrust imbalance at high altitude if the rocket motors were not perfectly aligned. This was not happening in practice, and the large lower ventral stabilizer was having a negative dihedral effect that impaired stability in flight at high AoA. Wind-tunnel tests indicated that the lower ventral stabilizer could be omitted on high-altitude flights without appreciable risk, despite a 27 percent decrease in vertical tail area.

Bob Rushworth made the first flight with this configuration on October 4, 1961 with encouraging results, and in 1962 the lower ventral was usually left off. Range was slightly increased and re-entries at Mach 6 were eventually flown. In all, 126 out of the 199 X-15 flights were made without the lower "wedge." However, it was retained for Joe Walker's spectacular April 30, 1962 flight in which he reached 246,700ft.

BROKEN GLASS AND BALLISTICS

The X-15's small cockpit canopy allowed a minimal glazed area that was barely adequate for its main function – allowing the pilot to locate and land on the selected runway area. Bob White flew the second aircraft to 217,000ft and Mach 5.21 on October 11, 1961, marking the first occasion on which the ballistic control system was used fully. On re-entry the external pane of his left windshield panel developed a pattern of cracks and he watched "little slivers of glass falling away." On the next flight, when he became the first pilot to exceed Mach 6 (shouting "Go, go, go!" over the radio), the right-side outer pane (made of alumino-silicate) shattered as he wound down to Mach 2.7. Fearful that the left panel might also fail, he contemplated jettisoning the thermal paint-covered canopy at subsonic speed and trusting to his helmet faceplate for protection. With some close-formation help from a chase F-104, he was able to land. Part of the windshield frame had expanded and buckled under severe heating, so titanium was used to replace the Inconel-X at that point, removing the hot-spot. White did find that the ballistic controls worked well, although peroxide consumption was higher than expected. A transfer system was therefore installed in all X-15s to feed the ballistic controls with any remaining peroxide from the XLR-99's turbo-pump reservoir.

Neil Armstrong's April 20, 1962 flight was planned for Phase VI, testing the MH-96 system in ballistic flight up to 205,000ft. Control was maintained very effectively, although he had recourse to the turbo-pump peroxide reserves for the thrusters. When he attempted a pull-out on re-entry at 116,000ft, X-15-3 began a slight climb and remained

Bob White was flying X-15-2 on November 6, 1961, decelerating through Mach 2.7 after the first-ever Mach 6 flight, when the right outer windshield panel shattered. A similar fracture occurred to the left window on October 11. If both windows had been lost the impossibility of landing would have necessitated ejection. Extreme heat also distorted the canopy on a later flight, damaging the seal. An incursion of hypersonic air into the cockpit would have incinerated the pilot in seconds. (NASA)

above the atmosphere, resisting Armstrong's attempts to initiate a turn. At Mach 3 and 100,000ft it "skipped" past Edwards AFB and continued south for 45 miles before it began to slow and enter the atmosphere. Eventually he managed to turn back towards base, knowing that there were no contingency plans for a landing on the "wrong" (south) side of Edwards. The convoy of emergency vehicles began a high-speed, 12-mile dash from the usual Runway 18 at the northern end of the lake area to Runway 35 at the southern edge. Armstrong was able to make a normal landing after a record overshoot that fellow pilot Milt Thompson called "Neil's cross-country flight."

As the X-15s achieved progressively higher speeds and altitudes in Test Phase VII the pilots' workload also became more demanding. Disorientation in those conditions, especially at high g in a climb, during which no horizon could be seen, was a particular hazard. Bob White found this during several flights in mid-1962. In a ballistic control test on June 12, for example, he wanted to push the nose down despite a correctly indicated 32 degrees of pitch because he felt that the aircraft was still trying to climb more steeply or over-rotate, and he was sure that he should be seeing the horizon. As a result he undershot the 206,000ft altitude by 21,400ft. A similar situation occurred nine days later, but White's undershoot was reduced to 3,300ft and he went along with what his instruments and ground controllers were telling him.

However, on July 17 he was scheduled to zoom to 282,000ft in X-15-3 but the MH-96 malfunctioned just after launch. Determined to continue, White reset the system's circuit breakers and pressed on, a little more steeply than prescribed. Combined with an unusually long motor burn, the ascent took him up to 314,750ft, with an

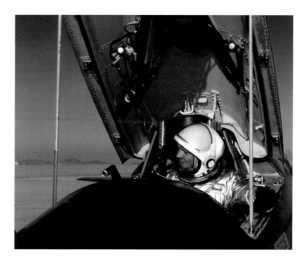

Neil Armstrong suited up for the check-out flight of X-15-3 on December 20, 1961. The new MH-96 system was evaluated on this flight. Installed only in X-15-3, MH-96 worked well and in 1966 it enabled the aircraft to reach 360,000ft while the other two X-15s were restricted to 265,000ft. The red, retractable helmet headrest in the canopy roof helped the pilot to avoid straining his neck when the rocket-plane experienced high-g deceleration during re-entry. A 16mm camera is fixed on the right side of the canopy. The air-conditioned cockpit and the pressure suit were pressurized at 3.5psi with nitrogen. (AFFTC)

Bob White with X-15-1. He specialized in precise X-15 landings within 15ft to 100ft of a selected touchdown point – a skill that was subsequently emulated by pilots of the Space Shuttle "glider," including Fred Haise. In high-g situations the A/P22S-2 suit squeezed the pilot's lower abdomen and legs, forcing the blood back to his heart and brain to prevent black-outs, and leaving red marks on his body. (AFFTC)

overshoot of 32,750ft – the entire cruise altitude of a typical airliner, but only ten percent of his own altitude. In a speeding X-15, one second's extra burn time translated into 4,000ft altitude and a one degree error in climb angle could add another 7,500ft.

Even this overshoot was exceeded on November 1, 1966 when Bill Dana, aiming for a 39-degree climb to 267,000ft, actually pulled 42 degrees and soared to 306,900ft – an epic excess of 39,000ft. His day was spoiled by accidentally knocking his checklists from their kneepad clip while reaching over to turn off the XLR-99 in weightless conditions. Dana lamented, "I had 27 pages of checklists floating around the cockpit with me – it was like trying to read Shakespeare sitting under a maple tree in October during a high wind. I only saw one instrument at a time for the remainder of the ballistic portion of the flight."

White's aircraft thereby became the first to fly above 300,000ft, and he was the first X-15 pilot to qualify for astronaut's wings, having exceeded an altitude of 50 miles. After briefly enjoying the view of San Francisco Bay from that distance, he managed to make a turn without overshooting, arriving at the "high key" point of his return to base at 80,000ft and Mach 3.5. It was an international record-breaking flight for a rocket-powered aircraft within the atmosphere, and the X-15's only official record. It is unlikely to be bettered as the atmosphere ends at 328,099ft, and a new record would have to exceed White's by three percent, reaching 328,098ft.

White, Crossfield, Petersen and Walker were all called to the White House the following day (July 18, 1962) to receive the 7ft-high Robert J. Collier Trophy from President John F. Kennedy for "invaluable technological contributions to the advancement of flight and for great skill and courage as test pilots of the X-15."

JACK'S BAD LUCK

Aerodynamic heating flights continued into 1962, and Jack McKay made one in X-15-2 on November 9, aiming for 125,000ft and Mach 5.55. Immediately after launching from the NB-52B he checked that his throttle was fully open, but the engine was only generating 35 percent power due to electrical control problems. There were no contingency statistics for landing at such low power, although McKay might have been able to reach Edwards and get rid of his propellants in time to land. Instead, he shut down the sick XLR-99 and turned towards Mud Lake. He jettisoned as much of his heavy propellant load as possible and began to let down, but the landing flaps were inoperative.

The extra weight of fuel and the lack of flaps increased McKay's landing speed to 292mph, 46mph above normal, and the left rear skid gave way, causing the left wing and tailplane to cut into the lake's surface and swing the aircraft sideways, turning it over on its back. McKay anticipated the peril of being trapped inverted in a potential fireball or dying from lack of oxygen, or even nitrogen inhalation, and he jettisoned the canopy as the aircraft began to roll

over. Unfortunately, this meant that his helmet was driven into the dry mud runway, crushing several of his vertebrae, making him an inch shorter and causing years of constant pain.

Fortunately, Mud Lake had a designated rescue crew, an H-21 helicopter and a fire truck on standby. As they approached the crash site within a minute, the groundcrewmen were driven back by leaking ammonia, which their breathing masks could not cope with. The helicopter pilot, Capt Paul Balfe, was trained for this situation and he fanned the fumes away with his rotor. Rescue personnel were then able to dig a pit under McKay, extract him from the cockpit and put him in the paramedic-equipped C-130, which quickly arrived from its rescue-flight orbit between Edwards and Mud Lake. For once, the APUs kept running, albeit after the crash.

Although McKay was back at work five weeks later, and eventually made another 22 X-15 flights, he had sustained lasting damage that would hasten his death in 1975. The X-15-2's incredibly strong airframe was repairable despite such severe damage. Six months after the rocket-plane's recovery and inspection, it was decided to rebuild and modify it so that the X-15-2 would reach the original design speed of Mach 6.5 and go further to Mach 8.

Altitude-biased flights continued into 1963 and Joe Walker made the highest flight of the program on August 22 after a preparatory attempt on July 19 when he overshot an intended 315,000ft ceiling by 31,200ft. He reached 354,200ft, travelling at 5,600ft/sec, on August 22 and re-entered at 45 degrees, travelling at more than a mile per second and pulling 5g on the level-out at 70,000ft. In 11 minutes and eight seconds Walker had covered 305 miles horizontally and 67 miles vertically, although his NASA astronaut status took many years to be confirmed. It was his last X-15 flight, and no further flights were made until October 7, when USAF pilot Capt Joe H. Engle made his familiarization flight during which he upset the NASA ground personnel with an unauthorized slow roll in X-15-1.

Engle's two years on the X-15 included 16 flights, with one at Mach 5.71. In 1966 he would become the youngest NASA astronaut recruit. His X-15 missions went well, although on August 10, 1965

Flap failure spoiled Jack McKay's attempt to recover X-15-2 onto Mud Lake on November 9, 1962. Severe damage to the right wing, horizontal stabilizer and landing gear can be seen. (NASA Dryden)

Damage to X-15-2's rudder and fuselage is revealed as it is lifted onto a flat-bed truck. By June 25, 1964 it was flying again as the modified X-15A-2. (NASA Dryden)

the MH-96's yaw damper channel failed at 271,000ft. Rather than converting his flight to low altitude as the rules demanded, Engle reset the damper but then had to reset it about every 10–15 seconds, 21 times in all, for the rest of the flight.

Milton O. Thompson also joined the program in October 1963 for 22 months, the ninth pilot to do so. A former US Navy pilot in World War II, he had flight-tested the B-52 and M2-F1 and M2-F2 lifting body vehicles. The first of Thompson's 14 flights in the X-15 was made on October 29, 1963 at a time when most of the basic research program had been completed and various extension projects were being formulated. Many senior figures, including Paul Bikle, questioned the value of the continued expense and risk of prolonging what had been a very successful venture. However, the cancellation of the projected Dyna-Soar on December 10, 1963 helped to re-emphasize the X-15's importance. It also validated the decision to rebuild X-15-2.

The program continued into the next test phase, taking the total number of X-15 flights to 120 – including two hours above 3,000mph – by the end of 1964. New NASA experiments and data-recording equipment were installed. X-15-3 (56-6672) had a new, sharper leading edge fitted to its vertical stabilizer, while extra stiffening was added to the X-15s' structures - all bore the stress-marks of hard use, with obvious wrinkles and skin repairs. NASA stated that each post-flight refurbishment of an X-15 cost $270,000, but it anticipated that the program would continue into 1968, with the first and third aircraft retiring in 1967.

NEXT PAGES PILOTED SPACEFLIGHT

Maj Bob Rushworth's mission on June 27, 1963 in X-15-3 tested stability with the lower ventral stabilizer removed and deployed an experiment to measure the Earth's background ultraviolet radiation and another to measure the infra-red exhaust signature of lox- and ammonia-fuelled rocket motors. More importantly for Rushworth, his maximum altitude of 285,000ft, at which he relied on the ballistic control system to maintain stability, qualified him as an astronaut.

NAA X-15A-2 66-671

On November 3, 1965, during Flight 2-43-75, X-15A-2 undertook the first flight with external tanks. It was also the only launch made from the Cuddeback Dry Lake area. Bob Rushworth tested handling with the empty tanks aboard and jettisoned them at Mach 2.25, although the lox tank's parachute did not deploy – the only time this ever happened with the tanks. The jettisoned lower ventral fin also landed without a parachute on this occasion.

FASTER PHOENIX

The X-15s' slightly excessive weight had held them back from their intended maximum Mach 6.5 speed, and additional power was needed for sustained flight at this speed and above. The rebuilt X-15-2, redesignated X-15A-2, was intended to test a new, NASA-developed air-breathing Hypersonic Research Engine (HRE), or "scramjet" (supersonic combustion ramjet) capable of operating at 100,000ft in temperatures of 2,400 degrees F. Its fuselage was extended, with a 29in plug at its center of gravity to provide space – with upper and lower windows – for optical scientific equipment, requiring all electrical wiring and rigging to be spliced to cover the extra distance. It could also house a liquid hydrogen tank, planned (but not

ABOVE
The disintegration of X-15A-2's tires during the August 14, 1964 landing coincided with a subtle alteration to the "Beware of Blast" notice near its ballistic control nozzles. The aircraft's black finish helped to radiate frictional heat, or "emissivity," which could reach 1,000 degrees F over the flying surfaces and nose so that they started to glow red. Inconel-X was, in any case, very dark in appearance, and it became blue-black as it heated up. (NASA Dryden)

ABOVE RIGHT
Scorched nose-gear components after Bob Rushworth's August 14, 1964 recovery, when the small "scoop" door at the rear of the main gear door inadvertently opened and extended the undercarriage unit. The shallow grooves made by the tireless nose-wheels show the hardness of the dry lake surface. (NASA Dryden)

installed) for the Marquardt (later Garrett AirResearch) ramjet that was to be suspended under the ventral fin.

More obviously, gigantic external propellant tanks were attached to the lower fuselage sides, increasing the propellant load by 70 percent but adding only 60 seconds' burn time. This in turn required the addition of new tanks in extended side-tunnels for the storage of more hydrogen-peroxide turbo-pump fuel and a new spherical helium tank behind the base of the vertical stabilizer for extra pressurization gas.

The extra length meant repositioning the X-15 attachment points on the NB-52 pylon to keep the vertical tail in the correct carriage position. Additional weight required stronger landing skid struts that were 6.75in longer to allow for the 30in-diameter ramjet nacelle under the ventral fin. The nose-gear was strengthened and mounted 9in lower to give a correct landing attitude. After the first flights the ballistic control system was removed as the revised aircraft was prioritized for speed rather than high altitude.

Other modifications included a "Skylight" hatch behind the cockpit, with two 20in-long upward-opening doors through which experiments and cameras could be raised on a small elevator to do their work. An ultraviolet stellar photography experiment was carried on five flights in 1962, although the data obtained was limited due to the difficulty in maintaining the precise altitudes that the sensors required. The canopy had new eliptical, triple-pane windows to withstand higher temperatures without the previous expansion and cracking problems. Although most of the X-15-2 airframe had survived the November 1962 crash, the outer right wing had been bent upwards as it cut into the desert and a new, detachable panel had to be fitted. Initially, this was seen as a chance to fit interchangeable outer panels to test a range of structural materials, but only the first panel was ever used and fully instrumented.

After wind-tunnel testing of the basic configuration, the rebuilt X-15A-2 was completed on February 25, 1964. It was only 773lb over the intended launch weight of 49,640lb, of which no less than 32,250lb comprised propellants – 18,750lb internally and 13,500lb in the external tanks. Bob Rushworth performed its captive flight on June

15 and the check-out flight ten days later, in which he hit Mach 4.59 and an altitude of 83,300ft, with Jack McKay as NASA-1 controller. The aircraft's handling characteristics were essentially unchanged, including a tendency towards directional instability.

On August 14, Rushworth was scheduled to check a stellar photography experiment (for the Orbital Astronomical Observatory Satellite project) in the "Skylight" bay and he accelerated to Mach 5.23 and 103,300ft. Seconds later he heard a loud bang and the aircraft "began to oscillate wildly and I couldn't seem to catch up with it." He reduced speed, engaged the dampers and became aware of smoke in the cockpit. The sound reminded him of the nose-gear extending, and he deduced correctly that the nose-gear door had opened, releasing the undercarriage unit into the scorching 1,000 degrees F slipstream.

Still travelling at Mach 2.5, he decided to go for Edwards. Twenty miles from the runway Joe Engle's chase F-104 caught up, and he reported that the nose-gear was indeed down and the tires looked "pretty scorched – I imagine they will probably go on landing." Rushworth's fear that the whole nose-gear unit might collapse, causing another fuselage fracture like Crossfield's in 1959, proved unfounded. Apart from the burned-off tires, there was no major damage. McKay experienced a similar incident in X-15-1 on May 15, 1963 when the nose-gear scoop door opened at Mach 5.2 and the nose-gear unit was twisted 20 degrees to the right. His tires failed on touchdown and large chunks of rubber flew past the cockpit.

Rushworth's close shave was yet another incident caused by aerodynamic heating, which had made the fuselage expand faster than the release cable restraining the nose-gear in its bay, pulling the cable tight. When the nose-gear door also expanded the extra

The X-15A-2 is loaded beneath NB-52A 52-003 – note the rocket-plane mission tally on the fuselage of the Stratofortress – ahead of its November 3, 1965 flight by Bob Rushworth, the first with (empty) external tanks. It has reshaped cockpit windows and an open "skylight" sensor bay behind the cockpit. Landing with the tanks aboard was impossible, so safe jettisoning was essential, and this had to be done below Mach 2.6. The aluminum tanks had recovery parachutes to deposit them in the Edwards bombing range area for reuse. (AFFTC)

The dummy Hypersonic Research Engine (HRE) with the 40-degree nose-cone mounted to X-15A-2's ventral stabilizer on October 3, 1967. (NASA Dryden)

The X-15A-2 in October 1965. The two massive external tanks were a controversial topic among engineers, particularly concerning the weight imbalance between them. The left tank, weighing 1,150lb empty, contained 793 gallons of lox and three helium bottles, taking its weight to 8,920lb. In the right tank 1,080 gallons of anhydrous ammonia increased its 648lb empty weight to 6,850lb, giving an imbalance of around 2,000lb, and consequent trim problems. (NASA Dryden)

load on the undercarriage uplock bent it, releasing the nose-gear. A less severe failure occurred on the September 24 X-15A-2 flight when the small nose-gear scoop door opened at Mach 4.5. Some redesign of the nose-gear and a check during what NASA called a "low-speed flight" (Mach 4.66) resolved the problem.

Rushworth was unlucky yet again on his next flight, on February 17, 1965, when the right landing skid suddenly extended at Mach 4.3, causing alarming sideslip until he could restore stable flight at subsonic speed. As before, an uplock bent by excessive heating was to blame. Rushworth expressed his frustration by giving the aircraft a kick as he left it.

He was in the cockpit again on November 3 for the first flight test of the external fuel tanks, jettisoning them successfully at Mach 2.25 and 70,600ft. His brief five-minute flight showed that roll stability with the tanks attached was poor, although longitudinal control "wasn't quite as bad" as he expected. Tank separation was successful, but only the ammonia tank was recovered in repairable condition. However, the project's aim of using a ramjet to reach Mach 8 was undermined on August 6, 1965 when Secretary of Defense Robert S. McNamara withdrew funding. Other improvements to the X-15 fleet continued, including a Lear-Siegler instrument panel with vertical-scale displays for X-15-3, together with a third landing skid under the lower ventral to permit higher landing weights and provision for wingtip-mounted experiment pods.

Poor winter weather at Edwards delayed testing the new experiments until May 1966, and on July 1, Rushworth, on his last X-15 flight, made the first test flight of the X-15A-2 with full external tanks. He knew that if fuel transferred from only one tank the aircraft would roll beyond the corrective capability of the flying controls. The difficult task of measuring fuel flow accurately for this purpose was handled by a pressure transducer system, and immediately after launching he jettisoned a small amount from each tank to test the system. NASA-1 control reported no flow from the ammonia tank, however, leaving Rushworth with no option other than to blow the tanks off.

Maj William "Pete" Knight became the tenth X-15 pilot from September 1965, serving on the program for almost three years. With early experience on the F-89D Scorpion, ten years' test flying at Edwards, and 253 F-100 Super Sabre combat missions in Vietnam, he was chosen for the Dyna-Soar project before moving to the X-15. Bob Rushworth was replaced by Maj Michael J. Adams, whose familiarization flight was on October 6, 1966, but it was curtailed by the collapse of the forward ammonia tank bulkhead in X-15-1, stopping the motor and forcing him in to Cuddeback Lake for a successful landing. A fuel jettison valve had been inadvertently opened during the pre-launch checks, creating unbalanced pressure in the ammonia tank. Later the same day an engine in Adams' T-38A failed, causing him to make a second emergency landing.

In 1967, a wet winter again delayed flights until March 22, when Mike Adams tested the additional third landing skid. "Pete" Knight's June 29 flight was aborted by the old problem of APU failure when both units shut down, causing the XLR-99 to close down above 80,000ft. Soon afterwards he lost all electrical power, leaving him with only hydraulics from the one APU that he managed to re-start. "Everything quit. By this time I was heading up and the airplane was getting pretty sloppy," he reported. "Once I thought I was level enough I started a left turn back to Mud Lake. I made a 6g turn all the way around. I used some speed brakes to get it down to 25,000ft. On the final I was getting pretty tired of that side-stick, so I began to use both hands, one on the center stick and one on the side-stick. The airplane was a little squirrelly without the dampers but not really that bad. It was a nice landing as far as the main skids were concerned, but the nose-gear came down really hard."

Knight's ground run was more than 9,000ft. It was one of many occasions when piloting skill and experience saved an X-15 although the "textbook" might have recommended ejection. With no radio or radar transponder operating on the aircraft, some at the control room thought Knight had done just that until Bill Dana in Chase Two caught sight of him heading in to Mud Lake. Paul Bikle called the recovery one of the most impressive events in the program. Knight's electrical problem was traced to one of the on-board experiments overloading an APU – a recurrent problem.

BEATING THE HEAT

Hypersonic speed and heating in excess of conditions experienced by manned aircraft were anticipated for spacecraft, and many designers focussed on silicone-based elastomeric coatings as ablative heat-shields. They were lightweight, easy to apply by spray or in sheet form and could

Inviting comparison with an oven-ready chicken, the X-15A-2 receives its pink ablator. Application began with intensive scrubbing with solvents after taping all joints and gaps. Pre-molded ESA-3560-IIA silicone covers were glued onto all leading edges. MA-25S ablator was then sprayed on, varying the thickness according to the required level of protection. After hours of curing, the surface was sanded to within ±0.20in of the required thickness. White Dow Corning wear-resistant sealer was then sprayed over the pink MA-25S, essential warning notices were painted on and gap-sealing tape was replaced with strips of MA-25S-1. The process took about six weeks. After a flight, damaged ablator was sanded off and replaced using kitchen spatulas to smooth it out. "Pete" Knight was among the pilots who swore that he would "never fly a pink airplane." (NASA)

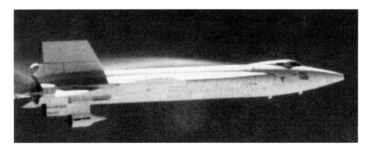

"Pete" Knight makes the August 21, 1967 flight with full ablator, the 20-degree HRE and a Hycon camera. His windows became partly obscured by ablator fragments. (AFFTC)

X-15-2 tested the dummy ramjet with a 20-degree nose-cone on May 8 and August 21, 1967 at speeds approaching Mach 5. (Mach 5.5 equates to a mile per second.) Acceleration was dramatic, increasing by 90mph per second and requiring a steep climb after launch to prevent the X-15 from over-speeding and causing structural damage. Forrest Petersen compared it to a catapult shot from an aircraft carrier. At launch the X-15 was a 33,000lb aircraft with 57,000lb of thrust, but as fuel burned off the ratios changed to around 15,500lb weight and up to 60,000lb of thrust. (NASA)

be patched up when they melted or eroded ("ablated") under extreme heat. In its planned speed increase to Mach 8, X-15A-2 would encounter exponential temperature increases that would require a prohibitively expensive redesign of the heat-sink areas of the airframe. Ablative protection and insulation seemed a possible solution, and limited tests were conducted on X-15-1 in 1961.

Various products were tested, with Thermalog 500 as the initial selection. It proved to be somewhat water-soluble and took too long to heat-cure, so in 1964 Martin MA-25S was specified instead, although continued flight testing revealed problems with adhesion to the aircraft's surface. Removal of charred or damaged ablator required scraping and soaking in solvents. Complete protection of the airframe was essential, especially in "hot spots" such as the area under the nose where temperatures could reach 1,750 degrees F at Mach 8. It was also noticed that loosened ablator fragments would move aft in the slipstream and stick to the aircraft further back. They could cover a windshield, prompting thoughts of a disposable outer windshield pane, or boundary-layer air playing onto the windshield. Eventually, the idea of a hinged metal eyelid that was closed over one pane during the high-speed flight section, when outside vision was not essential, was adopted.

Because MA-25S was impact-sensitive when exposed to liquid oxygen and could detonate with minimal force, it was decided that a white outer protective layer was also needed in case of small spills during refueling. Bob Rushworth flight-tested the new finish on selected areas of X-15A-2 on May 19, 1966. On the leading edges, which were the hottest areas, another material called ESA-3560-IIA was used. It was pre-molded from fiber-reinforced elastomeric silicone

NEXT PAGES MACH 6.7

This plate depicts X-15A-2 on its final flight on October 3, 1967, piloted by Maj William J. "Pete" Knight. It has the full MA-25S ablator coverage and white Dow Corning DC90-090 protective layer. The external tanks were dropped at Mach 2.4 and the dummy ramjet (with 40-degree nose-cone) ejected itself when heat-damaged. Although this particular flight recorded the fastest speed ever achieved by the X-15, reaching an unofficial Mach 6.7, hypersonic heat damage to the ramjet and the modified ventral stabilizer indicated that faster speeds were unlikely to be achievable with adequate safety.

Heat damage to the ventral stabilizer of X-15A-2 after its Mach 6.7 flight on October 3, 1967. (NASA Dryden)

material, and similar pieces of pre-molded MA-25S were supplied to cover fasteners, seams and access-panel lines. The first flight with a full ablator coat took place on August 21, 1967 when "Pete" Knight reached Mach 4.94 with only minor burns to the finish. The X-15A-2 was also fitted with a dummy ramjet in place of the lower ventral fin – ominously, the heaviest charring occurred on the leading edge of the ventral fin.

Knight flew a second test on October 3, this time with ablator, external tanks, a revised dummy ramjet and the windshield "eyelid." He accelerated away at a 35-degree pitch angle, correcting a roll to the left due to the heavier external liquid-oxygen tank. Reaching Mach 2.4 and 72,300ft, he jettisoned the tanks (which were recovered and repairable)

With ablator covering the two-piece "eyelid" over its left window and filling the ballistic ports (unused on later high-speed flights), X-15A-2 displays the full heat-proofing treatment on August 4, 1967. (NASA Dryden)

and rapidly accelerated to a peak altitude of 102,100ft. Knight leveled out and reached Mach 6.7 (4,520mph) before engine shut-down. He had just set an unofficial speed record for winged aircraft, beaten only by the Space Shuttle in 1981, but the X-15A-2 had sustained damage in the process.

Shock waves from the ramjet's nose spike, interacting with the ventral fin, caused a tenfold increase in local heating that burned off the ablator, melted areas of the ramjet, detonated three of its explosive jettisoning bolts so that it fell away prematurely, and destroyed wiring and pressure lines inside the ventral stabilizer. Luckily, the speed brakes survived, making landing possible. Although the ablator worked well generally, local temperatures in areas like the ventral fin were 2,400 degrees F – twice the guaranteed limit for Inconel-X. The aircraft was repaired and returned to Edwards in June 1968 for ground tests, but it never flew again.

There were nine more flights remaining, but the 191st on November 15, 1967 was the worst. Michael Adams, scheduled to carry several experiments including one to measure the ultraviolet exhaust signature of rockets, took X-15-3 to 85,000ft, where electrical arcing interference from a right wingtip pod "bow shock standoff measurement" experiment tripped out the MH-96 dampers and the ballistic controls. It also misled the flight control system into thinking it was at a lower altitude, where the ballistic controls were not automatically engaged, rather than at 266,000ft, where Adams was still trying to start up the experiment.

Distracting, inaccurate INS data began to appear on his panel and INS "fail" lights illuminated. He misread an attitude indicator, which could be switched to read either sideslip or pitch and bank error, and

Michael J. Adams with X-15-1. He was killed in X-15-3 on November 15, 1967 in the program's only fatal accident. (NASA)

NAA X-15-3 66-672
Edwards AFB, California,
April 28, 1967

On April 28, 1967, during Flight 3-58-87, Bill Dana flew this aircraft without its lower ventral fin in place. The aircraft had wingtip pods for an accelerometer experiment, a third landing skid and an extended Inconel-X leading edge to the vertical stabilizer. It also had the Cold Wall panel experiment affixed to the rudder to test the resistance of the surface to sudden heating when an insulating panel was ejected at high speed.

was therefore unaware of a sideslip to the right which was at 15 degrees and increasing as he descended through 130,000ft, where he began to fly sideways and soon entered a hypersonic spin. The Master Warning light on the upper left of his instrument panel lit up, but there was no indicator at NASA-1 (manned by "Pete" Knight) to warn that Adams' heading was totally wrong until he announced, "I'm in a spin." There was also no official advice available for that situation but the aircraft recovered itself at 120,000ft and entered an inverted 45-degrees dive at Mach 4.7, descending at 160,000ft per minute as the chase pilots headed off to the most likely emergency landing lakes.

Adams' chances of pulling out of the dive were negated by another electronic MH-96 fault, which made the aircraft pitch up too steeply and soon induced rapid, severe pitching oscillations as it entered denser air. Any attempts by the pilot to correct this were automatically blocked as it hurtled downwards at Mach 3.93, oscillating in pitch with 12g vertical aerodynamic loads and 8g lateral loads – far beyond its structural limits. The X-15-3 disintegrated at 62,000ft, crashing into Death Valley with Mike Adams still aboard.

A key item for the accident enquiry board was the cockpit camera that filmed the instrument panel and Adams' strenuous actions to try and save the aircraft. It was found after a week of searching, but without its film cassette. Engineers managed to calculate the trajectory of the small cassette by studying wind drift at altitude, and a search party was eventually able to locate it in the desert two weeks after the crash. Its rain-damaged film revealed that Adams must have misinterpreted the ambivalent attitude indicator instrument, but it also became clear that he had suffered from severe vertigo on this and previous occasions. It was a medical condition that had not been subject to rigorous screening up to that time, and pilots were reluctant to admit a tendency towards vertigo as it could affect their career prospects.

The awful loss of Adams and the X-15-3 confirmed Paul Bikle's

conviction that the program should end due to high costs and unacceptable risks, although he had hopes for a delta-winged derivative. It had originally been planned to run 100 flights only in order to cover the research needs. In December 31, 1967 it was agreed that the USAF/NASA operation would continue until December 1968, using only X-15-1. Eight more flights were made by "Pete" Knight and Bill Dana – the last two pilots assigned to the program – and the 200th, and final one, was scheduled for December. However, after ten attempts that had to be aborted either due to bad weather or maintenance problems it was abandoned.

Flight 199 on October 24, 1968 was the X-15's last stand. Dana reached Mach 5.38 and 255,000ft carrying, like several of the last-phase flights, an experiment to track the ultraviolet signature of a climbing Minuteman ballistic missile to see whether tracking hostile missiles would be possible. Sadly, coordinating the flight-path times

X-15A-2, with external tanks and the 40-degree HRE, sets off on Flight 2-53-97 – its fastest, but final, flight. (NASA)

This view of the X-15A-2 on display at the National Museum of the USAF shows the bulk of the external tanks and the wide, wedge-shaped, vertical stabilizer. (Michael Benolkin)

of the missile and the X-15 proved impossible on nine occasions after $700,000 was spent on the attempts.

Other experiments had continued to explore high-altitude sky brightness as part of star-tracking research for Lockheed U-2 navigation, definition of the horizon at various altitudes for the Manned Space Flight project, and ablative finish research for the Saturn space venture. Although each aircraft had averaged only ten hours' flying time (130 hours including "captive" time on the NB-52) during the whole program, all showed fatigue from extensive testing – statically as well as in extreme flight conditions – throughout the nine years of the project. Milt Thompson commented that, "we wore the airplanes out testing them in preparation for flight." It had been an unprecedentedly fast aircraft, exceeding Mach 6 four times and Mach 5 on 108 occasions.

X-15A-2 was certainly looking worn out in November 1968, with many components removed and extensive work required even to prepare it for museum display. X-15-1, in better shape, was requested by the Smithsonian Museum in 1971 for the museum's Milestones of Flight Gallery. X-15A-2 was refurbished and put on display, with its external tanks and "ramjet," at the National Museum of the USAF in 1971, while the third aircraft's remains lie buried somewhere under the Edwards desert. The two carrier aircraft soldiered on for the NASA lifting body program, and NB-52B "Balls 8" finally retired in November 2004 after 40 years as a flying launch platform. Although it had made 1,051 flights totaling 2,440 flight hours, it still had the lowest total of flying hours in the entire B-52 fleet.

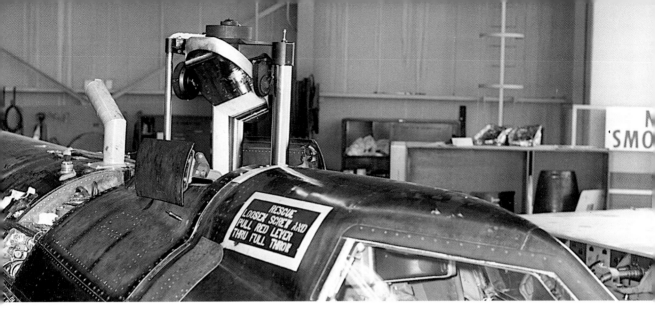

CHAPTER FIVE

WHAT MIGHT HAVE BEEN

The Western Range Launch Monitoring experiment extends from the "Skylight" hatch of X-15-1. Several flights were also generated for NASA's meteorite dust collection experiment based on the assumption that an X-15 could fly undamaged through a meteorite shower and collect dust in a pod on the left wingtip that opened to admit the fragments before they were burned up in the atmosphere. From October 1964 six missions brought back small samples, but they were contaminated by the ballistic thrusters' emissions and useless in the laboratory. On several occasions the pod opened due to electrical surges, temporarily destabilizing the aircraft. (NASA)

Interest in developed versions of the X-15 continued throughout the project, and there were requests for additional aircraft from 1958 onwards, although all were rejected by NASA and the USAF. Many suggestions were far-fetched, including a proposal in 1966 to launch a delta-winged version from the back of an XB-70 Valkyrie bomber to give it a Mach 3 start to its flight on launch. The cancellation of the XB-70 after two were built and the many potential hazards of the venture soon curtailed this suggestion.

In 1960 the X-15 itself was put forward as a launch vehicle for NASA/USAF RM-89 Blue Scout rockets or Viper IC sounding rockets for upper atmosphere research at altitudes above 380,000ft. Versions of the Blue Scout rocket, launched from rails extending from a pylon beneath the X-15 at 200,000ft, would have powered small satellites into space. It was also seen by the USAF as a means of testing weapons delivery from space and as the first X-15 operation away from Edwards, with the NB-52/X-15 launching from Cape Canaveral, in Florida, and landing in the Bahamas – presumably on a normal runway, with the alternative "wire brush" landing skid surfaces that were also suggested. This project also died during discussion, as did an even more fanciful notion of using two X-15s. flying in formation to provide in-flight refueling for the USAF's projected orbital Aerospaceplane at Mach 6!

An earlier proposal, in response to Sputnik I, was for the 1957 X-15B to be used as a manned orbital vehicle. This enlarged, two-man version of the X-15 was part of Gen Curtis LeMay's plan to ensure that a USAF pilot would be the first man in outer space, expressed in Project 7969

which included the option of Dyna-Soar. It would also have served as an astronaut training vehicle, capable of landing on normal runways.

Although it was replaced by the Project Mercury ballistic capsule idea, orbital X-15B was a serious proposal for a three-stage vehicle using a Navaho rocket with a G-38 booster as a first stage, a single Navaho for the second stage and the X-15B as the third. It would have used a Rocketdyne XLR-105 Atlas motor developing 75,000lb of thrust instead of the XLR-99, its Inconel-X skin was thicker (or replaced by more heat-resistant Rene-41 alloy) to withstand increased re-entry heat and its propellant tanks were enlarged. The two Navaho booster stages would have taken the X-15B up to 400,000ft, from where it could accelerate to 18,000mph under its own power, make three Earth orbits before re-entry and return to Edwards, or possible crew ejection over water.

The proposal was followed in 1968 by Harrison Storms' revised version, using an X-15B on top of a Saturn rocket booster with an ICBM-type second-stage using eight Jupiter boosters to enter a distant

The projected XB-70A/X-15 launcher combination to increase the latter's potential top speed. (Rockwell International)

NEXT PAGE   X-15B – WHAT MIGHT HAVE BEEN

Among many plans for advanced X-15 versions was one that mounted the proposed two-seat X-15B on Navaho rocket boosters to give it suborbital, or potentially even orbital performance. Although Harrison Storms foresaw this project putting an X-15, loaded with experiments, hundreds of miles above the Earth, there was no interest from NASA or the USAF. The X-15B would have had a ball nose, thicker Inconel-X structure and a 75,000lb-thrust Rocketdyne XLR-105 Atlas rocket motor with three Navahos. The first two Navahos would have burned out 80 seconds after launch, having provided 830,000lb of initial thrust.

Washburn Laboratory's "Startracker" Ultraviolet Stellar Photography Experiment under the "Skylight" hatch of the X-15A-2 produced the world's first ultraviolet star images in August 1966. (NASA)

Earth orbit, or a lower orbit with a heavier scientific payload. The entire launch assembly would have generated 1,500,000lb of thrust. Project Mercury soon sidelined the X-15B and Storms correctly predicted that "we may be left out in the cold" with orbital projects. The "Q-ball" nose did, at least, appear on the Saturn rocket. Perhaps the most intensively researched advanced X-15 concept centered on the use of a thin delta wing modification to X-15-3, also using the MH-96 and other modifications made to X-15A-2. The suggested changes to the aircraft reflected the growing popularity of highly swept delta wings for hypersonic cruise vehicles requiring more lift than the small wing of the basic X-15 could provide. Specifically, flight-testing such a wing was seen as the only way of establishing its heat-transfer characteristics in turbulent air conditions.

NASA Langley recommended nickel- or cobalt-based corrugated webs for the wing structure, with refurbishable leading edges. NASA Ames Laboratory wanted several removable test panels on the airframe to study heat-sink behavior and a range of replacement nose sections ahead of the nose-wheel well to carry different instrument combinations and study various nose geometry configurations. External propellant tanks could be carried in a 10ft "stretch" to the fuselage, and a permanent thermal protection system would be applied, rather than ablators. Maximum speed would be around Mach 7, with short dashes at Mach 8, and the NB-52 launch system would be retained (limiting the wingspan of the delta X-15), with research flights continuing until 1973.

Some earlier flights were in support of the US supersonic transport project (SST). Milt Thompson's May 21, 1964 flight in X-15-3, with a razor-sharp leading edge to the rudder, was supposed to simulate a Mach 3 SST cruise. In fact, the X-15 did not like to travel so slowly and the engine flamed out when Thompson throttled back. The project was undermined by both time and cost. By March 1967, when contracts for the "delta" X-15 conversion would have been issued for a retro-fit during 1968, USAF support for the whole X-15 program was already diminishing. The estimated $29.75m cost came at a time when Apollo, NASA's most expensive undertaking, was limiting other projects.

NAA continued wind-tunnel testing with Langley, refining the wing to include a 76-degree leading-edge sweep, wingtip fins for stability and provision for the ramjet nacelle under the ventral fin, as before. There was much discussion about the shape and composition of the wing leading edge and of thermal protection, some of which linked directly to the company's preliminary work on the Space Shuttle. The "ball nose" was no longer required as there would be few high-altitude flights at high AoA. In effect, a new fuselage was proposed with extended tanks, an extra instrument bay, a re-located nose undercarriage in a new nose section and mounting points for the delta wings. The XLR-99 was uprated to 83,000lb thrust and an early fly-by-wire control system was a possible addition. USAF support was still lacking, however, and the loss of X-15-3 put an end to the delta X-15 as well.

The team of Williams, Becker and Feltz produced NASA's series of rocket X-planes and the Space Shuttle. The unique X-15 was undoubtedly the most successful of the USAF/NASA rocket-plane programs, although it helped to accelerate spaceflight progress so fast that by 1991 Neil Armstrong could describe it as "a primitive pathfinder in the conquest of space." As a research platform it was the only reusable craft that could carry useful instrument loads beyond the atmosphere, and it could have reached beyond 400,000ft but for the difficulty of re-entry from that height. With its MH-96, the X-15

A September 1967 version of the delta X-15 based on the X-15-3 fuselage with corrugated wing surfaces, additional outboard vertical stabilizers and an X-15A-2 ramjet below the ventral stabilizer. (NASA Dryden)

pioneered sophisticated adaptive flight control systems that would soon become standard in high-performance aircraft.

The X-15 also became the main source of hypersonic research data, which was vital to the safety and rapid development by NAA of the Apollo spacecraft and the Space Shuttle. The latter had similar approach and landing characteristics to the X-15 according to Joe Engle. It introduced reaction control systems, essential to all later space travel. HASTE (Hypersonic and Supersonic Thermal Evaluation) was a mathematical modeling process for aerodynamic heating that originated in the study of hot-spots on the X-15 airframe and it allowed the Apollo designers to use less heat protection on their spacecraft. They also opted for silica tiles rather than time-consuming ablator application. They were surprised by the X-15's revelation that skin heating was more severe than expected at high altitudes and less of a problem lower down. ICBMs, reaching 15,000mph and descending from an altitude of 500 miles, would reach temperatures high enough to melt their warheads, so thermal protection data was vital.

X-15 operations also provided both NASA and the USAF with some useful experience of full-pressure flight suits and of the biomedical effects of weightlessness and high-g acceleration. The rocket-plane also introduced a number of innovative structural materials and techniques for hypersonic craft. Much of this technological data, recorded in more than 750 research reports, is still unused, but remains available for future projects.

Most spectacularly, the X-15 was the first aircraft to exceed Mach 4, Mach 5 and Mach 6, doubling its top speed within 15 flights. In fact, the rocket-plane would probably have been capable of reaching Mach 7 if the ramjet had been successfully integrated. Crucially for the space program, as the "first of the spaceships" and last of a line of NACA rocket-powered research aircraft, it was the first craft to take men to the edge of space and show that safe re-entry was also possible. In 1955 many scientists believed that NACA's suggested "space leap" of a few minutes to explore weightlessness and extra-atmospheric flight was still far-fetched and futuristic, possibly realizable in the next century. The X-15 team's achievement of these goals by 1961 was therefore all the more remarkable.

FURTHER READING

BOOKS

Anderson, John and Passman, Richard, *X-15 – The World's fastest Rocket-Plane*, Smithsonian Institution/Zenith Press, Minneapolis, Minnesota, 2014

Baker, David, *North American X-15 Owner's Workshop Manual*, Haynes Publishing, Yeovil, Somerset, 2016

Crossfield, A. Scott with Blair, Clay, Jr, *Always Another Dawn*, Hodder and Stoughton, London, 1961

Evans, Michelle, *The X-15 Rocket-Plane*, University of Nebraska Press, Nebraska, 2013

Godwin, Robert (Ed.), *X-15 – the NASA Mission Reports*, Apogee Books, Burlington, Ontario, 2000

Gorn, Michael H., *Expanding the Envelope: Flight Research at NACA and NASA*, University Press of Kentucky, Kentucky, 2001

Guenther, Ben, Miller, Jay and Panopalis, Terry, *North American X-15/X-15A-2*, Aerofax, Inc., Arlington, Texas, 1985

Jenkins, Dennis R. and Landis, Tony R., *Hypersonic*, Specialty Press, North Branch, Minnesota, 2003

Lockett, Brian, *Balls Eight – History of the NB-52B Mothership*, Lockett Books, Goleta, California, 2015

Thompson, Milton O., *At the Edge of Space*, Smithsonian Institution, Washington, D.C., 1992

Tregaskis, Richard, *X-15 Diary – the Story of America's First Space Ship*, Dutton, New York, New York, 1961

Van Pelt, Michel, *Rocketing into the Future*, Springer-Praxis, New York/Heidelberg/Dordrecht, 2012

White, Robert M. and Summers, Jack, *Higher and Faster – Memoir of a Pioneering Air Force Test Pilot*, McFarland and Company, Inc., Jefferson, North Carolina, 2010

DOCUMENTS

Hallion, Richard, "On the Frontier – Flight Research at Dryden, 1946–1981," NASA Publications SP-4303, 1984

Heppenheimer, T. A., "Facing the Heat Barrier – A History of Hypersonics," NASA Publications SP-4232, 2007

Houston, Robert, Hallion, Richard and Boston, Ronald, "Transiting from Air to Space – the North American X-15," Air Force History and Museums Program, 1998

Jenkins, Dennis R., "X-15 – Extending the Frontiers of Flight," NASA History Office

Jenkins, Dennis R., "Hypersonics Before the Shuttle," NASA Publications SP-20000-4518, 2000

"X-15 Utility Flight Manual," USAF, Secretary of the Air Force, 1961

Love, James E. and Stillwell, Wendell H., "Technical Note D-185 – the Hydrogen-Peroxide Rocket Reaction-control System for the X-1B Research Airplane," Flight Research Center, Edwards AFB/NASA, 1959

INDEX

References to illustrations are shown in **bold**, with the caption page in brackets if not on the same page.